W9-BVB-316

# Praise for *Twitter for Good*

"#Twitter4Good is the quintessential handbook for Twitter newbies, social marketing pros, and curious executives alike. Claire packed this guide full of overarching principles, scalable models, practical tips, and real-world case studies, gleaned from an insider's perspective. She debunks the skeptics and clearly maps out how people, content, and technology come together to make a very real impact, 140 characters at a time."

> —@darbyDARNIT, Petri Darby, director of brand marketing and digital strategy, Make-A-Wish Foundation® of America (@MakeAWish)

"A marathon achievement! Packed with insights and wisdom. #Twitter4Good illustrates—simply and clearly—how Twitter can propel your business to completely new heights. ReTweet this!"

> —Raymond Nasr, early Twitter advisor and communications consultant

"Giving is important to us all, and #Twitter4Good shows how to best use this exciting technology to share your social passions."

> —@LAAGiving2, Laura Arrillaga-Andreessen, author, *Giving 2.0,* and founder, Stanford PACS (Center on Philanthropy and Civil Society) and SV2

"Twitter provides a direct line to your constituents, where through authentic engagement—listening, learning, conversing—you can build genuine relationships that drive real-world impact. Claire Díaz-Ortiz shows organizations how to make the most of Twitter to deliver maximum value for their organization and the world."

—@lauramansfield, Laura Adams, digital lead of sustainable business and innovation, Nike

"For most organizations, Twitter is a foreign language, feared and misunderstood. Claire Díaz-Ortiz has written the greatest translation that exists, turning Twitter into an effective and manageable tool for businesses around the world."

—@unmarketing, Scott Stratten, author, *UnMarketing*

"Every non-profit and social justice organization knows now that they need social media to support the work they do. What's still unclear for many is the 'how'—what to say, when to say it, and how to know if it's working. Claire Díaz-Ortiz removes the mystery of tweeting for good. Her nuts-and-bolts guide is indispensable for beginners and experts alike."

—@randomdeanna, Deanna Zandt, media technologist and author, *Share This!*

# Twitter for Good

## Change the World
### ONE TWEET AT A TIME

**CLAIRE DÍAZ-ORTIZ**

Head of Corporate Social Innovation and Philanthropy, Twitter, Inc.

**Foreword by BIZ STONE**

**JOSSEY-BASS**
A Wiley Imprint
www.josseybass.com

Published by Jossey-Bass
A Wiley Imprint
989 Market Street, San Francisco, CA 94103-1741—www.josseybass.com

Jossey-Bass books and products are available through most bookstores. To contact Jossey-Bass directly call our Customer Care Department within the U.S. at 800-956-7739, outside the U.S. at 317-572-3986, or fax 317-572-4002.

Wiley also publishes its books in a variety of electronic formats and by print-on-demand. Not all content that is available in standard print versions of this book may appear or be packaged in all book formats. If you have purchased a version of this book that did not include media that is referenced by or accompanies a standard print version, you may request this media by visiting http://booksupport.wiley.com. For more information about Wiley products, visit us www.wiley.com.

**Library of Congress Cataloging-in-Publication Data**
Díaz-Ortiz, Claire.
   Twitter for good : change the world one tweet at a time / Claire Díaz-Ortiz.
      p. cm.
   Includes bibliographical references and index.
   ISBN 978-1-118-06193-0 (cloth); ISBN 978-1-118-12083-5 (ebk);
ISBN 978-1-118-12084-2 (ebk); ISBN 978-1-118-12085-9 (ebk)
   1. Twitter. 2. Social networks. 3. Social change. I. Title.
   TK5105.888.D53 2011
   006.7—dc23

                                                        2011017846

Printed in the United States of America

FIRST EDITION
HB Printing   10   9   8   7   6   5   4   3   2   1

*To José, amor.*
*To Sammy, mwenda wazimu.*
*To Lara, in payment.*

# Contents

# Foreword

In 2008, James Buck, a young photojournalism student attending the University of California, Berkeley, set off purposefully for Egypt to photograph citizens coming together in protest. A charismatic individual, it didn't take long for James to find lodgings and make friends. He hoped that over meals and coffee, his new friends would give news of upcoming protests—including locations—so he could be there to capture historic, iconic moments of civil unrest of Egyptian people protesting and share them with the world.

Although he established a strong network of friends, James found once there that he was not hearing about protests until after they had already taken place. He did, however, learn about the speed and efficiency with which these protests were assembled—and their powerful impact in various regions. He was also fascinated by how these assemblies so effectively disbanded, very often before the police showed up to make arrests.

Missing out on the action was of increasing frustration to James, especially given the limited time he had to accomplish his goals in Egypt. It seemed that an invisible and incredibly coordinated operation without a traditional hierarchy was operating all around him, and this compelled James to find answers. How were these protests so efficiently and effectively processed with so few arrests? What was the secret?

To get to the bottom of this mystery, James asked around, and his Egyptian friends answered him directly. "We all have mobile phones," they told him. "We are using them to access a free service that works over text messaging called Twitter." At that time, Twitter, Inc., had been incorporated for only one year, and most of Silicon Valley, not to mention anyone in the United States who had heard of the service, dismissed it as a useless waste of time.

On the advice of his friends, James signed up for Twitter so he could both receive and send Tweets—140 character text messages—on his simple mobile phone. He used it to chronicle his adventures in short bursts to his friends back at Berkeley, and more importantly, he started following the Tweets of several dedicated protesters. Within a few days, James received the kind of Tweet he had hoped for.

The Tweet told of a protest against the rise of food prices and dropping wages in Mahalla that had been discovered by Egyptian authorities and shut down. Peaceful protesters had been detained for too long. Tensions among family members and friends began to rise. Eventually these tensions flowed onto the streets, and they were not so peaceful. Molotov cocktails were being thrown and tires were set ablaze.

On April 10, James gathered his gear and headed to Mahalla, where the increasingly robust protests were gathering in strength. James was worried about getting arrested in such foreign surroundings, so he made sure he maintained a safe distance while he took photographs. That way, he figured he could not be associated with the protest. James's companion in Egypt looked him in the eyes and said that he had a bad feeling about that particular protest. They made a decision to leave immediately.

As they attempted to escape the area of activity, James and his companion were taken by Egyptian authorities. James quickly found himself detained in the back of a police car. Mohammed's "bad feeling" had turned into a very serious situation for the young student, and panic would have been a perfectly normal reaction. As luck would have it, the Egyptian police had not followed procedure—they had forgotten to take away James's mobile phone. Before the driver got back into the car to take him to a holding facility, James sent one of the shortest but most historic Tweets since the medium was created. The Tweet was only one word: "Arrested."

Cairo-based blogger Hossam el-Hamalawy at UC Berkeley was one of the first to see James's Tweet, and he helped spread the word of Buck's arrest. el-Hamalawy knew this situation could be dangerous, and he feared for James's safety. While James was being interrogated at police headquarters, word of his predicament spread quickly through Twitter and beyond. Soon, more friends at Berkeley knew, then the dean, then the Egyptian Consulate. Within a matter of hours, James was released from custody, and he sent out another one word Tweet: "Free."

When our small team in San Francisco first heard about the ordeal James endured and the role Twitter played in giving him an international voice, and ultimately freedom, our eyes were opened wide to the potential of what we had created. Long before we hired our first sales employee, we hired Claire Díaz-Ortiz to launch our Corporate Social Innovation and Philanthropy department. We were less than forty people at the time, but start-ups have a unique advantage to work the idea of "doing well by doing good" into the fabric of the company culture from the very beginning.

In 2011, I met with representatives from the Marine Corps of the United States of America. They wanted to learn how to use Twitter better during emergencies when they are called in to help victims of natural disasters. In those scenarios, every second counts. When there is an earthquake anywhere in the world, people are tweeting while the ground is still shaking. Those in a position to help want this information as soon as possible, and the right use of Twitter can help rescue workers and volunteers receive and send vital information.

At Twitter, we strive to make a positive impact in the world, but we cannot do it alone. If Twitter is to be a triumph, then it will not just be a triumph of technology, it will be a triumph of humanity. Claire Díaz-Ortiz was my first choice to lead our Corporate Social Innovation and Philanthropy team because she passionately believes that by democratizing activism, Twitter can help us all make the world a better place. She took weeknights and weekends to write this guide for helping non-profit organizations, foundations, and corporate brands running prosocial campaigns to determine how best to use Twitter.

I'm proud of Claire for her tireless effort and enthusiasm. And I'm proud of everyone who wants to take a step toward changing the world. People are basically good. When you give them a simple tool that helps them exhibit that behavior, they will prove it to you every day. Twitter has taught me this powerful lesson—among many other things. I hope Claire's work teaches you to use Twitter for the good you work so hard to achieve. Thank you for considering Twitter and good luck in all your endeavors!

*June 2011*                                                   Biz Stone
                                         Cofounder, Twitter, Inc.
                                       *San Francisco, California*

# Preface

I tweet from Twitter headquarters in San Francisco, helping non-profit organizations, foundations, and corporate brands running prosocial campaigns to determine how best to use Twitter to reach their goals. No matter the size of the cause, I help individuals reach their goals of social good on this unique real-time information network. *Twitter for Good* offers you these same tools to help you excel on Twitter.

My early days on Twitter took place from the Central Highlands of Kenya, where I ran Hope Runs (HopeRuns.org), a non-profit organization I cofounded. On a dial-up cell phone connection running painfully slow Internet access to the ground floor of my orphanage apartment, I sent my Tweets. Urging followers to learn about the effects of the HIV/AIDS epidemic on orphaned and vulnerable children, I tweeted about long afternoon runs spent holding hands with tiny Kenyan girls in discarded party dresses. I learned firsthand that you can tweet from anywhere.

Twitter has become easier than ever to use in the field. Every day, I work with individuals and organizations who are sending Tweets from the unlikeliest of places. Earthquake survivors sending Tweets from mobile phones in Haiti and Japan, volunteers tweeting information following volcanic eruptions in Indonesia, citizens tweeting in the midst of civil unrest in the Middle East, and anyone seeking to raise awareness for their cause around the world.

In my role leading social innovation, philanthropy, and causes at Twitter, Inc., I have developed a simple yet comprehensive five-step framework that teaches entities of all sizes to develop and employ innovative Twitter strategies. In *Twitter for Good*, I lay out the exact T.W.E.E.T. framework (Target, Write, Engage, Explore, Track) that I teach to individuals and organizations around the world. In-depth case studies, key best practices, and fast tips will show you how to simply and effectively create and execute your own Twitter strategy.

Specifically, this book will teach you:

- Why a Twitter strategy is so important
- Why you need a goal (I call this a Target) for your Twitter account, and how to craft one
- How to best broadcast your organization's good works to the world
- Why you can't get anywhere on Twitter if you aren't tracking your results

Along the way, I'll answer important questions typical of both newbie and veteran Twitter users. Questions like these:

- How many times a day should I tweet?
- What time of day should I send out my Tweets?
- Should I schedule Tweets ahead of time?
- How many followers is enough?
- Should I follow everyone who follows me?
- Should I edit my Tweets?
- Should my Tweets be questions or make statements?
- How do I know if I'm annoying my followers?
- How can I fundraise on Twitter?
- How often should I ask my donors for money via Twitter?
- How can I get another Twitter user to retweet my Tweets?
- Am I sending too many @replies?

And many, many more.

This book is for any for-profit or non-profit company that wants to make a difference and create a movement—whether with clean water in Ethiopia or with quality financial counseling in Seattle. Twitter is a tool for enabling individuals to reach their personal and professional goals, and the ideas in *Twitter for Good* can help anyone.

Finally, even if you enter with doubt, you will leave with confidence. Twitter is a simple, effective tool to help you start a movement, promote a cause, and improve your community. I will show you exactly how to use the service to reach these aims.

Most important, this book is for *anyone* who has a cause—no matter how big or how small. Twitter can help to drive world change, and it can do so from wherever you are—from a Silicon Valley start-up or a Kenyan orphanage.

By democratizing activism, Twitter can help us all to change the world. Here's how.

*June 2011*

Claire Díaz-Ortiz
*San Francisco, California*

# Introduction

We live in a world where more individuals have access to mobile phones than to clean water. It is this truth that shapes the greatest challenge of our age: How can technology solve today's most complex problems? How can we feed children, lift communities out of poverty, and create lasting, sustainable, positive global change with the high-powered technological tools at hand? The answer lies in the individual.

One criticism of Twitter is that its emphasis on the power of the individual does not effectively lend itself to wide-scale social change. Outright critics like Malcolm Gladwell contend that any one actor on an open-sourced information network has little ability to make a difference in the greater world. Reluctant adopters convey agreement.

Those on Twitter disagree. We say that this is where its strength is most clear. The root of Twitter's success is in its power as an open real-time information network. Twitter allows individuals to share minute-by-minute information about what is happening in their lives, their communities, and their world. Not only does it allow one to share *from* anywhere, but it also allows one to share *with* anyone.

In my early days tweeting via a mobile phone connection in Kenya (where there was no clean water in sight), I marveled that I was able to connect in real time with others half a world away.

**@ClaireD**                                    4 May 07 via im

no power, no water...only one short, short run...;)

http://twitter.com/#!/ClaireD/status/49919172

Five years later, millions of Tweets are sent this way each day. In this way, information leaps from person to person, from border to border, and change follows. The global growth of Twitter has also meant more opportunities for usage and more meaningful metrics proving its power. There's a reason why Twitter has been used increasingly in global crises—from Haiti to the Middle East to Japan and back again.

Technology is changing us, and we now have the unique opportunity to find innovative ways to use technology to help change the world. Twitter is one tool in this process. Just as Twitter lives on technology, however, it breathes with the people who use it. Twitter cofounder Biz Stone has said that the real triumph of Twitter is one of humanity, not technology. In this book, you will hear the stories of those who have made this technology come to life. As a simple platform where open communication reigns, Twitter elevates the individual voice; the strength of its platform is in the strength of the users.

In this way, individual activism *can* change the world.

# Be a Force for Good

**1**

One day at Twitter headquarters in San Francisco, I was doing a media training, learning to better convey my message and respond to common questions when speaking publicly. While employees around me had difficult and sensitive questions thrown their way about potential acquisitions and hiring statistics, I had it easy. "Tell me more ways that Twitter has helped people change the world," people typically ask me eagerly. Or, with interest, "What's your favorite story of using Twitter to help in a crisis?"

The trainer asked me what I wanted to work on. No one ever asks me hard questions, I told the trainer. And so he did.

"You say one of Twitter's operating principles is Be a Force for Good. But what on earth does that mean?"

Because broad questions don't merit vague responses, I dove in. I told one story of an individual using Twitter to change the world around her. One example that proved that the Twitter platform seemed built for social change from the beginning and that the way individuals are using it every day only maximizes its power. But there are many such stories I left out that day.

Think of this book as the complete response to that initial question. In these pages, I will teach you to be a force for good on Twitter.

## Corporate Social Innovation at Twitter

In my position leading social innovation, causes, and philanthropy at Twitter, and as the first employee to drive and shape such work at the company, I work on a daily basis to show non-profit and for-profit organizations how to use Twitter to make a difference. In my work, I help guide small non-profits, large non-profits, and big brands running cause campaigns in how to best use Twitter to reach their goals of social impact and world change. I believe it is not the *obligation* of an organization to engage in social change, but rather the *opportunity* an organization has to innovate in extraordinary ways, with this unique real-time information network. This book grew directly out of this work. As such, *Twitter for Good* is the definitive manual proving that individual activism via Twitter is a viable answer to world change.

Specifically, in Corporate Social Innovation and Philanthropy at Twitter, we work in three main areas to:

1. Support non-profit organizations and causes on Twitter
2. Promote cause marketing advertising initiatives
3. Carry out Twitter's internal philanthropic efforts

Our work breaks down as follows:

## Support for Causes

Twitter's operating principle, "Be a Force for Good," is the guiding principle of the service structure we provide to non-profit organizations and causes. The broad category of our non-profit support encompasses a variety of initiatives aimed at onboarding new non-profits and improving their experience on Twitter, including the following:

- Within our advertising platform, we offer pro bono programs for non-profits already engaged on Twitter. Promoted Tweets are a tool advertisers use to promote specific campaigns via Tweets on Twitter. The Promoted Tweets for Good program is an application-based pro bono program serving a number of non-profit organizations each year. We offer a second type of Promoted Tweets for Good ad hoc to organizations involved in crisis relief during times of natural disaster or civil unrest.

- We conduct regular talks and trainings to non-profits and causes who want to use Twitter better, based on the five-step T.W.E.E.T. framework explored in this book.

- On Twitter's Hope140.org, we compile an array of case studies, best practices, and past cause campaigns to help organizations better learn how to get started on Twitter.

- We work with organizations in the field of disaster response, taking advantage of Twitter's power on mobile devices to use our strategic partnerships to support humanitarian aid initiatives.

- Finally, we regularly bring speakers in to Twitter headquarters to better educate employees about innovative uses of Twitter in the world.

## Cause Marketing

Within the area of cause marketing, we support brands promoting prosocial or social good initiatives, generally through paid campaigns on Twitter's platform.

## Internal Giving

Within our internal philanthropic strategy we have spearheaded a variety of initiatives. Since 2009, we have worked with Room to Read, a non-profit organization supporting girls' education and library development in nine developing countries. We have mutually supported each other on a variety of initiatives related to literacy, including the creation

## What Is Promoted Tweets for Good?

Twitter launched our first advertising product, Promoted Tweets, in April of 2010. Much of the public didn't realize it, but Twitter launched Promoted Tweets not only with six big brands—including Starbucks and Virgin America—but also with two non-profit organizations: Partners in Health and Room to Read. Since that time, the Pro-Bono Promoted Tweets for Good program has served a number of key non-profit organizations with pro bono advertising on Twitter and has expanded to a secondary program featuring organizations serving Tweets in times of crisis. To find out more about Promoted Tweets for Good, visit www.Hope140.org.

## What Is Hope140?

Twitter launched Hope140 to help meet the needs of the growing number of non-profit organizations and causes on Twitter searching for best practices and training tools. At www.Hope140.org, you'll find case studies, examples of campaigns Twitter has engaged in to support causes, information on our pro bono advertising products, and a blog with the latest information and examples of causes on Twitter.

of a wine label for charity called Fledgling. We have also worked with a number of other organizations on ad hoc fundraising and Twitter-based awareness ca
ing (RED), Malaria No More, and the Ame

*Twitter for Good* provides a comprehensive manual that teaches organizations to help change the world using Twitter. Through working with hundreds of organizations, I have developed a simple five-step model called T.W.E.E.T. (*Target, Write, Engage, Explore, Track*), which uses case studies and examples to teach cause-based initiatives how to excel on Twitter's platform. *Twitter for Good* lays out this exact framework and will dive deep into the specific strategic steps needed to build and effectively promote cause-based campaigns. Case studies from organizations like the American Red Cross, Water.org, and Free the Children; eye-opening information about Twitter's own internal work on philanthropic campaigns; and how-to frameworks and models all are key elements of the text.

Although the focus of this book is non-profit organizations, social enterprises, foundations, and corporate entities running cause-based campaigns, many of the strategies explored apply to any entity that wants to make a difference in the world. Twitter is a tool for enabling individuals to reach their personal and professional goals, and the ideas in *Twitter for Good* can and will help anyone.

In speaking to thousands of individuals each year, the one question I receive most often is, "Where can I go to get more information about how to promote my cause on Twitter?"

This book—and Twitter's Hope140.org—are the answers.

*Twitter for Good* is designed as an engaging, case study–rich manual for innovative leaders in non-profit and for-profit sectors who want to use Twitter to achieve their cause-based aims. It is also the first work devoted to how causes and mission-based organizations can best use Twitter. It is a practical business book built around a targeted model for success, and it will provide you with the specific steps needed to excel as an organization on Twitter.

## The T.W.E.E.T. Framework

When I first began teaching organizations how to achieve their goals on Twitter, I used a variety of tips and strategies I had developed over time. Like most speakers, I sought to provide quality information in practical ways, and I always tried to create presentation outlines to reach my audience most effectively. I had spent thousands of hours learning about how non-profits and causes could best use Twitter, and much of these general resources could be found online—either at Twitter's website, www.Hope140.org; at www.Twitter4Good.com, the companion website for this book and its teachings; or at my personal website about causes and Twitter, www.ClaireDiazOrtiz.com.

However, when organizations asked me to give talks at conferences or provide hands-on trainings, I worked to craft ideas targeted to their specific cause. It was valuable, high-touch work. It was also not sustainable. As Twitter grew, the number of organizations on Twitter exploded.

I needed to find a way to reach more people, so I began to create more generalized presentations and trainings.

I was always interested in the retention level of audience members and workshop participants, and I was often dismayed to hear that typically only a few ideas really stuck. In my years as an attendee at conferences and workshops, I had seen the same thing. Despite the structure that presenters clearly gave to their presentations, the outline was not always obvious to the audience members. Without understanding and being able to recall the skeleton of the presentation, remembering the individual points presented was that much more difficult.

I realized that if my audiences were going to digest my message in one twentieth of the time it took for me to prepare it, it had to be as simple as possible. Only when they remembered the basics—and saw the importance of the one core idea—would they have interest in recalling the intricacies of what I explained or in seeking these resources later online at Twitter's www.Hope140.org.

Over time, I saw the need for a dedicated framework that any organization could easily remember and consistently employ. In its simplest form, an organization just needs to remember the five main things they should be thinking about when trying to excel on Twitter—T.W.E.E.T. (Target, Write, Engage, Explore, Track).

The T.W.E.E.T. framework works because it is simple. The jarringly obvious acronym serves as the absolutely easiest way for organizations to remember the five most important things they must do to stand out on Twitter. It has worked for hundreds of organizations, and I am confident that it can work for you as well.

Let's dive in.

# T (Target): Why Tweet?

The first step in the T.W.E.E.T. framework is identifying why you want to start using Twitter (or why you already are using Twitter) and what your organization hopes to gain from the platform.

It's time to ask yourself, out loud: "Why is my organization on Twitter?"

For many organizations, this simple question can be incredibly eye-opening. Some groups find that what they think they want out of Twitter does not match what they are actually getting. Some learn that the goal they once had either no longer serves them or has morphed into an entirely different one. And some organizations realize they have been drifting aimlessly without a strategy in mind. If your answer to this question is "I have no idea" or "Because someone set it up for me" or "Because everyone else is doing it," you know that you are likely wasting valuable time and resources.

Twitter can be an incredibly effective tool for all organizations, but to use it well you need to know what you hope to achieve by getting on in the first place. Whether you are just starting to use Twitter or are looking for ways to improve your current approach, you must come up with an effective, up-to-date **Target** for your Twitter account.

## The Three Most Common Targets

Although there are thousands of organizations on Twitter today, the vast majority use of one of three effective Targets, or goals, as their guiding principles. Specifically, here are the three most common goals I see organizations using for their Twitter accounts:

• *Information Accounts:* Information accounts are created by organizations that seek to be information hubs about a particular topic on Twitter. These accounts aim to be active, engaged accounts that serve as the go-to source for individuals seeking resources on a given topic—be it clean water, HIV/AIDS, literacy, event planning, or pet adoption. These accounts are likely quite professional in tone and risk seeming "stuffy" at times. Typically, several individuals (and therefore several voices) may take part in keeping the account active. Notably, the typical follower does not know who the author of the account is, as the accounts tend to remain impersonal.

See a list of examples of information accounts at
http://twitter4good.com/resources/information-accounts/

WEB

• *Personalized Accounts:* Personalized accounts are
created by organizations that want to use Twitter to put
a personal face on their organization. The organization
that chooses to make their Twitter account a personalized
account is often an older, more established organization
that has built a strong presence on Twitter and is now
turning to Twitter to either (1) find a new demographic,
or (2) transition an existing supporter base to a form of
new media. Personalized accounts are often not the sole
or primary accounts that an organization maintains, and
these may be in addition to a more professional, informative
account that focuses on important organizational
announcements. Although personalized accounts typically
come from prominent organizations and corporations that
are seen as highly successful or high-profile offline, there are
also many cases of smaller, more low-profile organizations
making a name for themselves through a very personalized
Twitter account. Personalized accounts are often managed
by one employee and imbue that particular employee's
voice in the Tweets.

Because social media managers are often younger
twenty- and thirty-somethings with more professional
instability, organizations can face problems when the
social media manager who had done so well personally
branding the organizational account moves onto a new
job. Given this, a better strategy for some organizations
with a personalized account is to maintain an overall

personal and casual feel on the account—showing the side of the organization not typically revealed in the monthly newsletter—without personalizing the account to one specific employee. We will explore this in depth later.

See a list of examples of personalized accounts at http://twitter4good.com/resources/personalized-accounts/

• *Fundraising Accounts:* Fundraising accounts are started by organizations that begin using Twitter in the hopes of opening up new doors for funding and support. They often have high follower numbers—or higher follower numbers than the average organization's account on Twitter—because of their quick ability to go viral. By asking for specific, tangible actions from the individuals reading their Tweets, they beg for retweeting—by both those who take up the call to action (by, say, donating or by signing a petition) and those who don't. They vary in success and in longevity, often peaking in certain seasons of the year. For this reason, fundraising accounts typically struggle with continuity of followers and long-term engagement.

See a list of examples of fundraising accounts at http://twitter4good.com/resources/fundraising-accounts/

Although your organization's particular Target may be different from these, these are the three most common goals I see successfully repeated again and again. Let's dig a little deeper to understand what is involved in each of the three main Targets and what organizations with each of these specific Targets actually look like.

## Information Accounts: Room to Read and Blackbaud

Like many individuals, I was first introduced to Room to Read through founder John Wood's bestselling book, *Leaving Microsoft to Change the World*, which tells the powerful story of how, after a chance vacation in the Himalayas, he left his high-profile career in technology to bring literacy to developing nations. On one level, his story resonates with anyone who has ever dreamed of leaving it all to start anew. The fact that Wood turned his initial experience collecting and donating books to a rural Nepali village into one of the most successful non-profit organizations of the last decade shows that such change—both personally and globally— really can happen.

Since 2000, Room to Read has had a strong history in the non-profit community as a global organization providing educational opportunities that change children's lives throughout Bangladesh, Cambodia, India, Laos, Nepal, South Africa, Sri Lanka, Vietnam, and Zambia. It got its start establishing small libraries in rural communities, and within ten years had established more than 700 schools and over 7,000 bilingual libraries worldwide— replete with no less than five million books lining their shelves. As of 2011, Room to Read also supported the education of nearly 7,000 girls through its scholarship efforts. Room to Read focuses on girls' education in particular. They believe that connecting girls (who later may become mothers) with educational opportunity has the greatest potential to improve education in communities worldwide.

As of 2011, Room to Read's programs have already reached more than three million children.

Twitter's belief in the open exchange of information fits well with Room to Read's mission to educate the world. Soon after I began working at Twitter in 2009, we started working with Room to Read on a longer-term partnership. At the same time, Room to Read decided to reevaluate their Twitter strategy.

To do so, they needed to better define their goals on Twitter and what they aimed to achieve through their efforts. With @roomtoread, they knew that they wanted to set themselves apart as an account that purveyed information about the importance of global education worldwide. Under the direction of Rebecca Hankin, director of communications, they had started their account on Twitter as an *information account,* tweeting about current events in global literacy, recent news from the countries in which they operated, efforts by their corporate partners, or initiatives on behalf of their local chapters. They believed that information was power, and they wanted their followers to find their Tweets as useful and informative as possible. Hankin focused on the organization's public relations, marketing, youth, social media, and online communication strategies; she was and is responsible for driving most of the tweeting efforts of the @roomtoread account. As she describes it, Room to Read's initial Target as an information account on Twitter had everything to do with global literacy: "Beyond providing education and literacy programs to children across the developing world, as an organization we also want to mobilize a global movement to break the cycle of illiteracy. Through our @roomtoread account, we have been able to educate our followers on critical issues related to global education—from timely news articles to commemorations of significant holidays like International Literacy Day—and share with them the work we and other non-profits are doing to provide innovative solutions." Hankin adds, "I'll admit, however, that our Tweets are not just about information—we also like to toot our own horn—telling our followers about our successes and how people can help. But I feel strongly that we don't want it to be all about us all the time, since everyone around the world can help contribute to our goal of changing the world by making sure every child receives an education."

Being an information account doesn't mean that @roomtoread shies away from other best practices, many of which we will explore in later chapters. Within their Target of being an information account, they also manage to make strides in many other areas. They built their initial list of followers by identifying the key players most relevant to them and then following them and engaging in conversations. They are good at cheering on other organizations and peers for a job well done, and use a popular hashtag #followfriday to do so. For newbies, #followfriday is a long-standing "meme" or viral digital concept encouraging Twitter accounts to tweet every Friday about good accounts they are following with the hashtag #followfriday. As @roomtoread found, it's a great way to find and share new accounts to follow from trustworthy sources.

See a list of popular memes at http://twitter4good.com/resources/memes/

WEB

Finally, although @roomtoread is an information account, they don't hesitate to tweet out important information that has more of a fundraising or personal focus.

Blackbaud, a for-profit social enterprise serving nonprofit organizations, had similar aims in starting up on Twitter as an information account. Since 1981, Blackbaud has focused on partnering with nonprofits to provide the solutions they need to have an impact on their local communities and the larger world. Blackbaud is the leading global provider of software and services designed specifically for nonprofit organizations, so establishing their brand as an information hub on Twitter fit in well with their company's aims. From the American Red Cross to Earthjustice and the International Fund for Animal Welfare, more than twenty-two thousand organizations use Blackbaud products and services. Melanie Mathos, public relations manager at Blackbaud, explained, "At Blackbaud, we don't think there's anything more important than helping nonprofit organizations do what they do even better, so we've develop[ed] solutions that allow them to stretch their resources further."

According to Mathos, although Blackbaud employees were on Twitter early, it took a bit longer for Blackbaud's corporate account to come online. "Many Blackbaud employees (being the tech geeks we are) started using Twitter in 2007, [but] the official Blackbaud account launched in September 2008. Our first foray into Twitter was from a personal development standpoint and we soon realized the benefits of bringing the 'official' corporate account online."

Ultimately, there were three main reasons that Blackbaud decided to establish a corporate-branded information account on Twitter:

1. *To have meaningful interactions with the community.* Whether community members be customers, prospects, partners, or nonprofit visionaries, Mathos had personally seen that Twitter breaks down barriers, and she wanted to ensure that Blackbaud's corporate account was benefitting from this phenomenon by using Twitter. "It does not matter if we are located on an island in Charleston, South Carolina (which we are)," she said. "With Twitter, we can share information and interact with members of our community around the globe in real time."

2. *To listen.* Mathos knew that using Twitter to listen would be a great way for Blackbaud to monitor their brand. In response to what they heard, they could be proactive with support, become aware of emerging issues and trends, gain valuable feedback on Blackbaud products, learn about new opportunities, and discover sales leads and prospects.

3. *To share information.* Twitter could also help Blackbaud to share information from their blogs about products, events and job openings. In time, it also proved to help them find free resources they could direct their non-profit clients to, and gave them a forum to hold social media contests to increase engagement. Mathos explained, "Twitter is

a thought leadership platform—not a used car sales lot. We believe that it is essential to contribute social capital and not just schlep product."

It's important to note that although Blackbaud's main Target identifies them as an information account, they do weave in small personal elements. "One thing that we think is important is that even the 'official' account has a personal feel. That is why we list the contributors to the account—@chadnorman and @melmatho—in the sidebar," Mathos explains, showing that within an information account it is definitely possible to maintain some personality.

### The Personalized Account: National Wildlife Federation, Stop Bullying, and Room to Read

Just as Room to Read decided to create an account known for its high-quality information about literacy, they also knew they wanted to add a personal element to their Twitter presence—and a more prominent one than the more limited way in which @blackbaud had integrated personality. To achieve this, they created a separate account for their CEO, John Wood, @johnwoodrtr.

Much of Room to Read's success is thanks to this dynamic founder. At the age of thirty-five, Wood was on a vacation to the Himalayas when a schoolteacher invited him to visit the local school. There, John observed that fewer than twenty books—backpackers' cast-offs, no less—were available for the more than 450 students itching to read them. Wood wanted to help meet the need, so he began collecting used books from friends and family and storing them in his family's garage, eventually bringing them back to Nepal. Since 2000 his work has expanded enormously, and he remains a dynamic, daily part of the organization, giving a face to the organization's mission.

By creating an entirely separate Twitter account for John that differentiated itself from @roomtoread, the organization was able to achieve multiple targets. @johnwoodrtr can give a more personal angle on his daily work, and the organization has even more Twitter angles from which to engage users.

I often recommend this strategy, as it allows for each account to have its own goal, without commingling them unnecessarily. Different followers will follow each account for different reasons, and any die-hard fans of the non-profit will simply follow both to hear two sides of the Room to Read story. Communications Director Hankin agreed that both accounts together "create a nice balance," adding, "It's also helpful that many of our local chapters are tweeting, and we have created a public list of those chapter handles, which adds a nice complement to our global tweeting."

In the beginning, though, it wasn't intuitive for the CEO. "For John Wood, it was hard to get him to start just because it was an unknown for him—and really, how often could he tweet when he is on the road 80 percent of the year? But I think he realized it actually has provided him with a nice platform to send out messages and information that he was already doing through longer, more private emails. In addition, it's been a great way for him to recognize so many of our corporate supporters who appreciate when the Room to Read founder takes the time to thank them via his feed. He also found it easy to tweet while on the road from his mobile device, and he's even started having fun with it. Nowadays, John totally embraces tweeting and sees the value in it—for both building his brand and the Room to Read name. I think his Tweets also make clear that it is, in fact, John himself tweeting—not just him retweeting Room to Read's messages."

John Wood agrees, outlining several reasons why he believes having his own Twitter account is so important.

> Why do I do my own Twitter feed, versus just letting @roomtoread tell the world what we're doing? Partially because I think people want to know what a founder is thinking. People may follow @twitter to hear the official news, but they also will pay attention to whatever they can learn from @ev and @biz. It gives them a different perspective. @roomtoread is great, and I love what my team posts, but most of it is very official. With @johnwoodrtr you get all the crazy stuff that happens to me during my "perpetual global road trip"—what inspired me, what pissed me off today, a random act of kindness I witnessed while traveling, or simply a TwitPic of a child reading a book in a remote library in the Himalayas. For instance, I posted a YouTube video of a bright young girl in Zambia who is on a Room to Read scholarship and now in tenth grade, and I tweeted it out. Within ninety minutes, I got an email from a Twitter follower who read the Tweet, watched the video, and then emailed me to say he would fund her *entire* university scholarship. As if that's not incredible enough, keep in mind that I am doing most of this from rural Zambia on a BlackBerry, and we're completely

changing a girl's life forever via this technology from the middle of the bush in rural Africa.

And it's not like sending an email [newsletter], because to be frank I'd feel guilty sending a mail saying "Hey, we just got a new $100,000 donation from a banker in Hong Kong," to over six thousand people. I'd hate to add to their already full inboxes. With my Tweets, I know that I am only reaching people who have self-selected to hear from me. [When choosing which Room to Read Twitter account to follow,] ideally, it's not either/or, but both, because anyone who cares about education for the developing world will hopefully follow both. Finally, I simply want to make sure that no matter how big Room to Read gets, we can "keep it real," and this means that people will still hear from the founder in a candid, uncut way. Nobody writes my Tweets for me. They are from the heart, they are me, they are what's going on in my mind (for better or for worse) at that moment. And with that, people can know more about what's happening at Room to Read, and on my insane global travels.

Many leaders agree with the value of maintaining personality. When I asked Alec Ross, senior advisor for innovation to the Secretary of State, how he balanced professionalism with personality on Twitter (especially in government work), he suggested that overly professional voices simply don't work on Twitter. "I think people tend to follow individuals rather than institutions, and if an individual voice sounds overinstitutionalized, it comes off as inauthentic." He continued,

> At a time when technology drives so much transparency towards everyone in our society, including our public officials, the challenge for us is to open ourselves up without diminishing the importance of our office or of our

undertakings. I think that can be achieved by mixing in a little communication about parenthood and football alongside freeing bloggers in Bahrain and meeting with heads of state. I think that the increasing power and ubiquity of our information networks reduces the degree to which we can mythologize public figures. When John Kennedy was president in the early 1960s there was something untouchable about him, something almost ephemeral. In this world of constant attention and the prying eyes of people with more than 5.1 billion mobile handsets, recording, transmitting, and amplifying every image, every moment, that sort of old-fashioned mythology is hard to maintain. For myself (a million miles from being a John Kennedy), I think it's impossible to even try to make real connections with people absent letting them inside a little bit.

John Carnell is also a fan of the personal voice. Carnell is the founder and CEO of Stop Bullying, an organization that started out of his own personal experiences with bullying in school. Stop Bullying uses social technology to keep costs low, including tweeting from their account, @bullyinguk. Carnell, who does the organization's tweeting himself, is a fan of the personalized account, reminding fellow nonprofits on Twitter that "YOU are just as important as the brand you represent! People want to learn a bit about you as much as the brand you are talking about, so [make sure to] tweet once in a while about yourself and sign your name at the end of the Tweet." Although the 140-character limit doesn't always make it feasible to add in your name at the end of the tweet as Carnell suggests (and this strategy could wear on your followers!), you can still bring in your clear personal voice.

The National Wildlife Federation (@nwf) faced an atypical challenge that led them to pursue a personalized account for their Twitter presence. Many organizations trying to make a name for themselves see Twitter and other forms of social media as a way to jumpstart this process. NWF, however, is different. As a seventy-five-year-old organization with over four million supporters, and the nation's largest conservation organization, the NWF's challenge was not to get on the map, but to bring their current group of supporters onto a new platform—Twitter.

Danielle Brigida works as the digital marketing manager for the National Wildlife Federation, but if you ask her, she's just a geek who loves using technology to help protect wildlife.

> I can't honestly say what it's like to be an up-and-coming nonprofit, but I tend to think we all have our challenges. What I like about Twitter is that you enter the scene on equal footing, and no matter your size, you have this account and it's up to you how you use it! I will say that older nonprofits generally have more processes in place that can impair real-time communication and marketing like Twitter. We are more cautious and can be set in our ways. The National Wildlife Federation was able to explore this space because our leadership was open to its potential and supported me to test things out. While larger nonprofits may not always move quickly to be early adopters, the National Wildlife Federation was one, partly because of my curiosity for technology and partly because many other people I have the pleasure of working with helped me by testing and joining sites. I often quote the Edelmen Trust Barometer (you have to see something three to five times to believe it) about why we started doing social media, but

quickly the mix of qualitative and quantitative benefits it brought showed how much of a range a tool like Twitter can have.

Within a year of getting onto Twitter, Danielle Brigida and the whole team built a strong following by using innovative ideas.

Even though I signed the National Wildlife Federation up for Twitter in early 2007, I didn't truly understand the functionality of the tool until close to 2008. My first Tweet was all HTML code. Once I got the hang of it, I was intrigued by the user base. I watched as writers, bloggers, and users from social bookmarking sites were updating their feeds with hopes to drive traffic to their blog or increase votes on Digg. Since I was an active user of sites like Digg and StumbleUpon, I immediately saw that Twitter was meaningful and unique—I just wasn't sure how we could translate that into something that benefited our work. At first, I used our Twitter feed to support environmental bloggers and stories that dealt with wildlife or other issues. By supporting like-minded people, and by connecting people and seeking out supporters, we were able to become a leader online and grow our audience. I also tested ideas like a "critter twitter" and tried different ways to engage our followers. I made the decision to follow people in return in order to show we were looking for real people and were open and accessible. In order to grow our numbers we focused on quality content [and] questions with a focus group feel, and also tried to be diligent with outreach and list cleaning. We joined a number of directories like Twellow .com and wefollow.com so that we could increase our findability. When I'm finding people to follow, I try to find people that will follow us in return. We also posted a list of all our staff on Twitter to make sure we were accessible.

Brigida especially loves the one-on-one contact that Twitter provides. "I want people to be able to direct message us and get an answer. I think this is something nonprofits are missing from a number of other sites, including Facebook. Twitter offers a great chance to converse with people if you want to establish a relationship with them."

Another way that NWF found to encourage existing donors and supporters on Twitter was to make their Twitter account a helpful, personal way to interact with families and to encourage them to bring their children into nature. Their *Ranger Rick* magazine for kids aged seven to fourteen had long been a hit, and NWF realized that Twitter could help bring some of the fun lessons and activities into the homes of subscribers on a more regular basis. Tweets encouraging families and kids to get out and enjoy the nature all around them with specific activity ideas proved popular:

10:31 AM Dec 23rd via CoTweet

**@NWF**

Too much holiday hoopla? Nerves frazzled?
Try a little family respite family outdoors:
http://bit.ly/eMNyqr

http://twitter.com/NWF/status/17935299568996352)

10:28 AM Dec 23rd via CoTweet

**@NWF**

Kids outdoors - six reasons parents tend to keep kids indoors -- and how to get over them:
http://bit.ly/aU433u

http://twitter.com/NWF/status/17934451300368384

Brigida explained how she came up with such fun games: "I always encourage people to have fun using social media. Writing a Tweet like a press release isn't always the best tactic, and sometimes it's just more effective to be yourself on these mediums while conveying a message that's relevant to the organization. Tweeting about coloring pages or wildlife facts is useful too, and in times of crisis, like the Gulf oil disaster, it was such a vital tool to elicit support and help from our followers." More generally, having a personalized account has helped @nwf achieve a number of goals, and Brigida says that ultimately, "We've been able to cultivate specific audiences and give programs more attention with their desired audience. I would say our strategy has worked much better than if we had limited staff or programs, because we can now support one another and diversify more responsibly."

Over time, donors have seen that Twitter doesn't replace the existing forms of contact they already valued with the NWF—including print and email newsletters—but rather adds to it, giving the NWF the chance to tell more of their story, more of the time. Tweeting has become a way to give a glimpse into a side of the NWF that had never been shown to the public on such a mass scale. Although some topics may not be big enough to make it into a monthly newsletter, now quick, fun, and interesting thoughts can be sent via Twitter to further engage supporters on a daily basis.

## The Fundraising Account: Twestival and Surfrider

The third main Target many organizations have when joining Twitter is to open a new avenue for fundraising, and many accounts on Twitter focus on fundraising as their main purpose. In discussing fundraising accounts on Twitter, I would be remiss not to mention Twestival and its founder, Amanda Rose. In 2008, Canadian entrepreneur Rose sought to prove that fundraising could work on Twitter. On February 12, 2009, she launched the first Twestival. A grassroots movement relying on volunteers all over the United States and in many foreign countries, Twestival 2009 held 202 volunteer-driven events and raised $264,000 for charity: water, the cause they chose as the focus of their efforts for the 2009 event. Twestival was a huge success in helping making clean water accessible to many, and the campaign showed the power of the individual to make a difference on Twitter. One of the clear tactics employed was allowing many different volunteer-led Twestival Twitter accounts to coexist to make maximum impact. "It was important we create a sense of community for the events around the world rather than just one person running it," Rose explained. "The best way to do that was to create a separate Twitter account like @ldntwestival or @madridtwestival. People are very loyal to their cities, and it translated online to Twitter by giving volunteers a voice and something to link to as a team."

Social media expert Beth Kanter has a similar example. As the author of Beth's Blog (http://www.bethkanter.org), one of the longest-running and most popular blogs for non-profits, and coauthor of *The Networked Nonprofit,* Kanter is no newbie in the field of using technology to have a social impact. She is also the CEO of Zoetica, a company that serves non-profits and socially conscious companies with top-tier online marketing services. Kanter worked with an interesting organization called Surfrider in their efforts to fundraise on

Twitter. Surfrider is a non-profit organization dedicated to the protection and enhancement of the world's waves and beaches. Like many non-profits, Surfrider fundraises on a chapter-based model. Organizations like Surfrider and Twestival—who fundraise via individual chapters—often deal with the issue of how much leeway to give individual chapters when they speak to the issues of the larger organization. Kanter explained to me that Surfrider took an interesting approach: "They were not afraid to let go of control and let their community spread their mission and message all over Twitter or Facebook because of the payoff—more supporters, more people signing petitions, etc." Ultimately, she said, "The issue is [one of] organizational culture and how much control the organization demands over everything versus building and nurturing a network that can inexpensively help you reach your goals." When it came to fundraising on Twitter, Surfrider was wide open to letting their chapters manage themselves and even brand themselves—meaning there were variations on the Surfrider logo based on which Twitter account (and which chapter) you were following. Kanter says, "One thing they are doing is encouraging chapters to use their new logo in any creative way they want—so they're balancing the brand dilution issue with network building." Ultimately, Surfrider (and Twestival) realized that the risk of brand dilution was less important than the payoff of maximum exposure. The freedom they afforded to the individual chapters to present themselves as they wished ultimately led to more accounts, more fundraisers, and more supporters.

## Which Target Is for You?

For some non-profit organizations, one of the three Targets just described will be an immediate and obvious fit. You may instantly recognize a personalized account, for instance, as the strategy to pursue. However, this is not always the case, and many non-profits simply aren't sure which Target is for them. If you are not yet sure which goal to pick, a simple process of elimination can help guide you.

If you are an organization new to Twitter, and you cannot decide which of the three Targets to choose, I recommend that you immediately eliminate the option of creating a fundraising account. A fundraising account should be a goal for only those organizations with a clear and present need and the urgent drive to carry it out. Of the remaining two goals, you should choose based on (1) the time you have to devote to your initial Twitter strategy and (2) the willingness of your organization to insert casual personality into the account.

Choose a personalized account if . . .

- You do *not* have a dedicated staff member who can devote a set amount of time to finding and culling important information about your cause—this is a clear indicator that you should rule out an information account as a possibility for your organization.
- Your organization is comfortable with personalizing the account—either as one individual branding it personally, or as multiple people contributing to show a personal face to the organization.

Choose an information account if . . .

- You definitely want to stay anonymous, are uncomfortable talking informally about your organization, and don't want to insert too much personality into your Tweets.
- You have a dedicated staff member, volunteer, or outside consultant who can devote time to finding and culling important information that your followers will deem valuable in relation to your cause and your area of expertise.

### Find a Role Model for Your Chosen Target

Once you have chosen a Target for your account, the next best way to ensure that you are proceeding well in developing your strategy is to identify a mentor to help show you the ropes on Twitter. This does *not* need to be someone you are actually in contact with. Instead, think of the mentor as a Twitter role model you can secretly follow and learn from. Modeling their efforts will help you jumpstart your own.

Read the top tips on finding a great Twitter role model for your case at http://twitter4good.com/resources/role-model/

### Account Target or Campaign Target?

Although we have been focusing on what it means to create a Target for your overall account, it is important to remember that individual campaigns will also need targets. If your overall Target is a personalized account, you would still need to address the fact that during certain months of the year your organization is on a fundraising push, and your Twitter account needs to clearly reflect that. You can do this while still following your overall Target.

For example, if your overall Target is a personalized account, your holiday fundraising initiative can have a subtarget of fundraising to reach donors with personal stories of volunteers at your organization working in your local community. When the holiday season is over, you can revert to the larger strategy of a personalized account, or create a new campaign for an entirely new springtime fundraising endeavor.

You can set your individual campaign targets in exactly the same way that you set your overall account Target, making sure to always remember your overall strategy. To plan the campaigns on your account, use a simple calendar or spreadsheet that plots out the months in the year. Most organizations already use similar documents in planning their major campaigns. On this calendar, write in all the individual Twitter campaigns you want to run throughout the year, and check each one to make sure it fits within the overall Target you have chosen for the account.

See an example of such a Twitter campaign planning chart at http://twitter4good.com/resources/plan-your-twitter-campaign/

**WEB**

## Keep a Flexible Target

Unexpected campaigns can—and should—also follow this rule. For example, @aircanada and @unmarketing are brands

that have clear Targets on Twitter. @aircanada is an information account for an international airline, and @unmarketing
is a personalized account written by Scott Stratten, speaker
and bestselling author of *UnMarketing: Stop Marketing,
Start Engaging.* However, both accounts have proved able
to develop different campaign-specific targets. When high-
profile blogger Catherine Connors (@herbadmother) sent
out a plea on Twitter to help her terminally ill nephew,
@unmarketing responded to the call, spearheading a massive
fundraising campaign from his Twitter account that raised
$25,000 in just twelve hours. @unmarketing was also ready
to vary his usual tweeting strategy when @herbadmother and
her nephew next needed him. After @herbadmother and her
nephew found themselves stranded in New York City after
Air Canada broke the nephew's wheelchair, @unmarketing
helped launch a firestorm on Twitter about Air Canada's
mishandling of the situation. Sending a flurry of Tweets,
he piqued the interest of thousands who began watching
the play-by-play. These thousands weren't just watching,
though; they were also tweeting. As Stratten explains, "One
of the things people need to understand about the Air
Canada incident is they [Air Canada] didn't listen until
people were screaming online ... We're all six years old; if
we don't think people are listening to our crying, we'll start
screaming (we just do it in ALL CAPS as grown-ups). All
people want is to feel they're being listened to, that their
concern is validated. The most powerful phrase a company
can utter is 'I'm sorry, I'll do what I can to fix this for you.'
You can't argue with that."

11:23 PM Aug 4th, 2010 via web

**@unmarketing**

Air Canada, you're making an incredibile day end horrlbly. Get Tanner hls wheelchalr replaced as promised that u broke

http://twitter.com/unmarketing/status/20353538292

Ultimately, @aircanada did apologize. Just as @unmarketing was able to change his Twitter strategy to participate in an important ad-hoc campaign or two, so was @aircanada—they became as personal as possible in their efforts to do relationship management and clear up the PR crisis, fixing the wheelchair and earning back the respect of thousands. Ultimately, setting an account Target is crucial, but so is having the flexibility to engage in specific campaigns with different Targets.

### What Will It Mean to Reach Your Goal?

Having an overall Target for your account is important, but you want to ensure that you are clear about how you will know when you are making progress in achieving your Target. We all love coming up with great goals, but on our path to completing them we often veer off and instinctively create new ones, ultimately never reaching the original targets we set. Take time to make sure you know what it will look like when you have succeeded in your first six months of implementation, and write down some of the results you hope to see. In Chapter Six we will look more in-depth at the

Track step in the T.W.E.E.T. model so that you can better understand how your Twitter strategy for your non-profit is progressing and whether it is achieving your aims. For now, it is sufficient to say that when choosing a Target, it is important to identify five *general* things you want to achieve with your Twitter account in the next six months. This doesn't mean you will close up shop on Twitter once you achieve them; rather, it will aid you in setting your next round of goals.

At this stage, these should be *generalized* goals. Many levels of specific metric points may exist within each goal, but for now these goals should sound more qualitative than quantitative. In Chapter Six, we will work on examining goals that are useful for all Twitter accounts to have and how to keep track. For now, though, I want you to set five generalized personal goals for your Twitter account. Here are some examples of potential goals:

- To build a following that is more responsive in providing feedback, and to find more quality followers
- To create separate accounts for all staff members and keep the main organizational account clean and professional
- To make sure that more locals attend the holiday fundraiser at the nearby community center
- To increase the reach of the organizational newsletter
- To draw more readers to the organization's website, where we provide great statistical information on our efficacy as an organization

Although these goals may seem subjective or hard to definitively measure, that is perfectly fine at this early stage. The important part is setting the Target and giving yourself some tangible ideas of what achieving this Target might look like six months down the line.

*To get started with your Twitter strategy:*

1. Set a Target for your account.
2. Find a role model to follow. (Remember: they don't have to know you exist!)
3. If applicable, identify separate campaigns within your organization (holiday toy pick-up, Thanksgiving fundraising, summer volunteer push, and so on) connected to your Target that you plan to promote.
4. Identify five generalized indicators that will let you know when you have reached this Target.

## Top Questions About the "Target" Step

Q: What if I choose the wrong Target for my organization's account?

A: This is a common fear, but it's an easy problem to remedy. If you've stuck to one Target or strategy for a few weeks and you find it's not working, simply change it. People following you may be confused at first, and you may lose some followers in the process, but in the long run this is by far the best thing you can do. Down the line, you'll be thankful you made the change when you did.

Q: How can I identify the Target choices of existing organizations on Twitter so that I can get a better feel for
what the three main goals look like in practice?

A: I often like quizzing workshop participants on what
Targets they believe particular existing non-profit
accounts have. By looking at twenty or so Tweets
from a given non-profit account, you can almost
always get a good idea of what that organization's
Target is. It can help you immensely to see what
that Target looks like in practice and which types
of non-profit organizations typically choose which
targets. I have given a few examples in this chapter,
but I encourage you to try your hand at spotting
some other organizations' Twitter targets. Take a
look at these accounts to start; you'll find a full list
on Twitter4Good.com.

> @amigos_americas
>
> @photovoice
>
> @acumenfund
>
> @oteshaproject
>
> @globalgiving
>
> @guidestarusa
>
> @miraklecouriers
>
> @mobiletransmike
>
> @kiva
>
> @naacp
>
> @skollfoundation
>
> @ridersforhealth

Q: Does the choice of which individual will tweet from my organization's account affect the Target I choose?

A: Absolutely! Unfortunately, when an organization is choosing the Target for their Twitter account, an individual who is not the social media manager or the person doing the tweeting will make the decision before speaking with—or even hiring!—the person who will be in charge of the tweeting.

This is particularly problematic for personalized accounts. The position of social media manager in many organizations today is often held by a younger—and thus more geographically and professionally unstable—employee. Combine this with the existing high turnover in the non-profit field in general, and you can immediately see that wedding the essence of your social media profile to one employee can be problematic in the long run.

The answer, however, is not to avoid setting the Target of a personalized account. Instead, be creative in how you use the personalized account. Some organizations—including one popular North American hotel chain—make this work by choosing an imaginary person—say, "Molly"—who does the tweeting for the account. Then, if the social media manager who served as "Molly" quits, whichever new social media manager steps in can assume the voice of "Molly."

Another strategy is to have a generalized personalized account that doesn't rely on one voice (even if one voice typically does your tweeting). You can see this with @charitywater, an account that personally connects with followers and invites a casual atmosphere—asking people what song they should play in the office, for example—but does so in a way that is not dependent on one particular employee doing the tweeting. Even if there is one specific employee (say, the social media manager) doing the tweeting, that doesn't have to be obvious.

# 3

# W (Write): Why You Should Tweet Like Kanye

After coming up with a proposed Target for your overall organizational account, and for the individual campaigns you want to run on that account, the next step is to start implementing your strategies. This step, *Write*, is all about extending information within your chosen Target so that others can learn what your Twitter account and your organization are all about.

## Joining Twitter, Getting Started, and Jumping on Mobile Tweeting

When I give trainings, there is a fine line between ensuring I give enough practical information on how to get started on Twitter and not overexplaining the basics of Twitter to veterans. Sometimes individuals suggest that I should walk through the actual signup process during the presentation.

In other presentations, however, I encounter questions from audience members that baffle me (and often the rest of the audience) with their nuanced understanding of the specifics of Twitter. For this reason, I will not focus on the how-to basics of getting started on Twitter in this chapter. Similarly, I will not walk through the exact steps of how to sign up for Twitter on your mobile device in this chapter. For these things, Twitter.com is your go-to resource. However, please keep in mind throughout this book that all references to tweeting and tweeting strategy encompass mobile tweeting as well—whether through a smart phone or in a country with fast follow (direct from SMS), as there are key benefits that tweeting on-the-go can offer organizations.

Now let's jump in to talk about what it means to craft your Tweet—to *Write* on Twitter.

## The Written Word—Or, What You Can Learn from Kanye West

For many new Twitter users, the hardest part of getting started is simply sending out your thoughts without overediting. The idea that millions may read your first attempt—and every attempt thereafter—can be a bit daunting. I promise you, it's a problem that every Twitter user has faced.

12:50 PM Mar 21st, 2006 via web

**@jack**

just setting up my twittr

http://twitter.com/jack/status/20

Time and time again, organizations send out a mild first Tweet, like, "Hello World! Finally figuring out this Twitter thing!" only to, days later, delete it and rewrite their first Tweet for posterity.

9 March 09 via web

**@GlobalCitizenYr**

Filling out our twitter profile.

http://twitter.com/#!/GlobalCitizenYr/status/1303238921

Is that wrong? Not at all. Sure, it would be ideal that we all craft something brilliant before tweeting it, but the reality is that such brilliance (usually) eludes us. The important thing is to get going, with whatever you write. Anne Lamott explains, in her superb guide to writing *Bird by Bird*, that putting your first words on paper—no matter what those first words are—is the most important step in the writing process. The creation of those bad first attempts is the key to eventually developing quality content. Though Lamott is referring to crafting a book, writing is writing, and when it comes to getting yourself into the habit of writing, tweeting is no different.

When giving presentations on how cause-based organizations can excel on Twitter, I often use famed Twitterer and rapper Kanye West as an example of what to do (much to the surprise of the audience). After all, what on earth can the prolific ramblings of a sometimes self-absorbed rap star have to do with the mission-based work of organizations? It turns out—a lot.

Although others might debate the merits of Kanye's tweeting abilities, I am a firm believer that there is no one who can better teach us all about the downsides of overediting ourselves on Twitter. Kanye shows the importance of putting out as much information as possible—especially during the early stages of your tweeting career, when you are just trying to find your legs on the platform. Kanye does not overedit his Tweets, and neither should you.

At Twitter headquarters, we often reference an important guiding principle called "fail fast"—the idea that you should try things, make mistakes, and do so quickly so that you can immediately jump back up and try again. The story of how Kanye got started on Twitter is not lacking in such spontaneity. One day in July of 2010, Kanye West and Twitter advisor and angel investor Ron Conway were spending some time together in the San Francisco Bay Area as Kanye learned more about social media. The story goes that Conway, ever the Twitter aficionado, asked Kanye why he wasn't tweeting to better connect with fans. Since they were in San Francisco, and Kanye was intrigued with Twitter, Conway asked Kanye to jump in his car and drive over to Twitter headquarters. As Conway told me later, "It was fun and interesting to host Kanye's visit to Twitter—where he learned that he could communicate directly to his fans for the first time . . . and he sure caught on fast!" Before meeting with Twitter management and employees and learning about Twitter, Kanye sent his first Tweet:

28 July via web

**@Kanyewest**

Up early in the morning taking meetings in
Silicone Valley

http://twitter.com/#!/kanyewest/status/19752583676

A minute later, he sent his second.

28 July via web

**@Kanyewest**

Lol I spelled Silicon wrong (I guess I was still thinking
about the other type of silicone ITS A PROCESS!! :)

http://twitter.com/#!/kanyewest/status/19755890378

Less than an hour after that, the Internet was abuzz with
his entry onto the information network. Although anything
Kanye said on Twitter might have gotten attention, it was
Kanye's particular breed of tweeting that really had people
hooked.

He was, in short, an immediate hit.

Saying everything he was thinking, without taking time
to spellcheck his writing or filter his ideas, his Tweets really
were a look into the complex, often funny brain of Kanye.
In talking about his couture tastes in couches, his international flight exploits, and—yes—his newfound love for
Twitter, he showed that his tweeting was authentic—
that this celebrity didn't have anyone doing his tweeting
for him.

Most interestingly, the flurry of Tweets didn't die down. In those early days, many speculated that Kanye was simply on an early Twitter high, and that his prolific, amazingly bizarre tweeting would soon give way to more infrequent, tame updates, as often happens with users (celebrity and non-celebrity alike). As of this writing, Kanye is still enthralling his followers with such witticisms and nonsensicalities as:

14 Nov

 **@Kanyewest**

I've finally realized as long as you use profanity when you talk about art and fashion it's better accepted!!!

http://twitter.com/#!/kanyewest/status/3977805188567040

12 Nov via web

**@Kanyewest**

Hotel robe got me feeling like a Sheik

http://twitter.com/#!/kanyewest/status/3087333352022016

4 Nov

**@Kanyewest**

I know that last tweet made no since hahaaa

http://twitter.com/#!/kanyewest/status/372659011452928

7 Nov via web

**@Kanyewest**

Even when I'm super tired I don't wanna let yall down... my fans are my family ... FANMILY!

http://twitter.com/#!/kanyewest/status/1290470974029824

To the pleasure of many, he's even inspired others—like Charlie Sheen—to emulate his everything-goes tactic. Jokes aside, what can worthy causes legitimately learn from Kanye? Although fans might argue that Kanye's wisdom is endless, there are three main things that Kanye teaches us about how to best convey information on Twitter. If organizations take these three things to heart, and add in a bit of both content and textual editing, they'll be well on their way to getting started with the Write step of the T.W.E.E.T. model on Twitter.

## Three Lessons for Organizations from Kanye West

- *Bite the bullet:* The time interval between Kanye's decision to join Twitter and his first Tweet was brief. Although Chapter Two encourages you to spend a bit more time in crafting your own organizational Twitter strategy, Kanye's enthusiasm to get going should be taken to heart. It's time to get started—no matter what the Tweet.
- *Let it all hang out:* Kanye doesn't edit himself, and (to some extent) neither should you. In the beginning, it's important to send out more information rather than less, and to be more personal than you might like. Erring on the side of overexuberance is a good bet for your first few days or weeks on Twitter, while you try different approaches to reach the Target you're aiming for with your account or campaign.
- *Fail fast:* In efforts to find your feet on Twitter, it's important to try different things (and to do so relatively quickly)

to see what your followers respond to. In Kanye's case, his strategy was an immediate success, so he ultimately never turned his back on his Target (a personalized account, if you're taking notes) to use Twitter as a running commentary on his eclectic brain.

Ultimately, when organizations first start tweeting they cannot be sure exactly how their planned strategy will proceed and how their new and growing list of followers will receive it. Kanye teaches us that the important thing is to get going—and to do so exuberantly. As you get started on Twitter, there will be a process of adjustment as you find your legs. The Twitter strategy you dream up in your boardroom may not be the one that most resonates with your followers, and adjustment will be needed. Although Kanye has found wild success with his bizarre tweeting (and in my opinion should never change his winning strategy), you want to evaluate whether things are really working for you. We'll touch on this in much more depth in later chapters, but for now it's important to point out that the reason for diving in is to find your legs as quickly as possible.

See a full list of some of the best Tweets of all time at http://twitter4good.com/resources/best-tweets/

## Using Multimedia in Your Tweets

Tweeting is not just about the written word. Text is powerful, but your efforts in multimedia may be much more likely to impress your followers. The launch of the new Twitter in September 2010 allowed for even better integration with multimedia, making it easier than ever to immediately have an impact with media in your Tweets. When Kanye TwitPics the targets of his online shopping addiction, his followers are more intrigued than when he just references it. Yours will be when you do so, too.

## Charity: Water and the Photo of the Day

As one of the most-followed accounts on Twitter, @charitywater was one of the first early causes on Twitter to truly prove that helping the world can be a popular topic on the platform. The history of charity: water and its charismatic founder, Scott Harrison, is an interesting one. Harrison was not your typical do-gooder in the clean water space. For years, the only watering holes this New York club promoter knew about were the ones that you had to pay a cover charge to get into. In a July 2009 piece by *New York Times* columnist Nicholas Kristof, Harrison famously said of his pre–charity: water self, "I realized I was the most selfish, sycophantic, and miserable human being. I was the worst person I knew."

But a trip to Liberia changed his life and set him on a new path to provide clean and safe drinking water to people in developing nations.

Harrison first leaped onto the Twitter scene in 2008, when his September birthday campaign raised an incredible $965,000 for clean water efforts. He caught the public's attention online and shared his dream of delivering clean water to those who need it most by posting catchy videos showing Manhattanites filling bottles to the brim with dirty Central Park water. Highlighting the campaign on Twitter—and sharing powerful videos—was crucial in making the campaign viral, and in the spring of 2009 charity: water was selected to be the recipient of the Global Twestival initiative led by Amanda Rose, where Twitter users came together to raise more than a quarter million dollars to dig wells in Ethiopia, Uganda, and India. Harrison explained to me, "charity: water's approach to Twitter is just an extension of our brand values: we try to be funny and inspiring; we value relationships with our supporters and care a lot about our communications. We love our Twitter audience and use it as our primary channel for news, updates, and insights into the inner workings of our organization."

Becoming one of the biggest accounts on Twitter doesn't happen by accident, and @charitywater has used a creative strategy to best gain followers and build a network of clean water activists and supporters on Twitter. One of their secrets—then and now—is powerful, personal media.

charity: water knows that getting you to care about a cause is all about getting you to see the problem, understand the problem, and feel the problem. charity: water uses high-impact media to do just that. First, they personalized their Twitter background with beautiful, powerful pictures of work they are doing in the field. Videos, which they place in their Tweets, convey their effective regular-guy-does-good message. Their photo of the day feature also gives followers a daily reason to remember the global efforts of charity: water and to share these accomplishments with friends.

The key to charity: water's success on Twitter has been their ability to translate their unique personality as an organization into their profile. Employing powerful media with a casual and interactive style, they have built a dedicated Twitter following with their Personalized Account. And when the masses follow charity: water, good happens in the world. In just over three short years, charity: water has raised enough money (more than $15 million) to bring clean and safe drinking water to more than a million individuals. Twitter influencers the world over have supported them as a result. Entrepreneur and Twitter investor Chris Sacca explains that being a supporter of charity: water is easy when they make their results so tangible: "I particularly appreciate organizations so efficient and accountable that they can show the exact impact of individual contributions. With charity: water, I can not only see the exact Ethiopian communities my donations have impacted, but I have even gone to Africa to visit some of those villages in person and see firsthand how transformational access to fresh water can be."

## UNICEF and Pepsi

The United Nations Children's Fund (UNICEF) has also found success with a similar multimedia strategy. The well-known organization has a more-than-sixty-year history of providing emergency relief to children, and it was an early adopter of Twitter, working hard to engage existing followers and encourage new ones. An important element of this was ensuring that @unicef was sending out quality information and content—no matter the source.

Matthew Cortellisi, senior global marketing specialist at UNICEF, explained that one of the challenges of the

UNICEF Twitter account lies in the fact that Unicef.org is not a destination website. Although many accounts rely on tweeting media links that direct back to their own frequently updated website, UNICEF doesn't have that option. Instead, they focus on tweeting quality content from many different sources and do not worry about the traffic it may (or may not) drive back to their website. Tweeting about fifteen times a week, they also rely heavily on multimedia in this practice. Video, for them, is a wildly popular means of attracting new followers and pleasing old ones. They aim to send out a video every week.

In contrast, Pepsi's Refresh Project shows what it means to pique the interest of the Twitter audience, drawing them toward a website to find more information or take action. Tara Roth McConaghy, executive director of the Goldhirsh Foundation, was once the COO of GOOD, Inc., and worked as a senior advisor on the Pepsi Refresh Project. Launched in January of 2010, the Pepsi Refresh Project aimed to take $20 million out of Pepsi's Marketing budget (separate from the Pepsi Corporate Foundation) and award it in grants to individuals, businesses, and non-profit organizations who sought to promote change in their communities. The project would later expand to include another $1.3 million for the Pepsi Refresh Project: Do Good for the Gulf. Twitter played a role in its success. McConaghy says, "Since the Pepsi Refresh Project is a democratic campaign about engaging online votes to win, non-profits, individuals, and businesses leveraged their voices and voting forces in a variety of ways, including through Twitter." Specifically, "Twitter allowed local stories to be broadcast across the nation and beyond to garner votes. Celebrities lent their support to promote innovative causes via Twitter." Ultimately, she says, "This type of campaign would not have been nearly as successful nor as popularly received or sustained without the power of Twitter and other social media."

## Cross-Platform Media and Tweeting via Mobile: Global Citizen Year and Tweeting from the Field

As evidenced with UNICEF, there is a reason that the mantra of any internet marketer or blogger—*content is king*—also applies to Twitter. On Twitter, however, that content can be no more than 140 characters.

One of the keys to the success on Twitter is learning how to leverage this small space to intrigue your followers. Ideally, you want your followers to both look forward to your real-time information updates and click through on the link or media embedded in your Tweet to learn more (as in the Pepsi Refresh Project). This is especially true when combining different forms of media and various platforms. Global Citizen Year (@globalcitizenyr) has been especially successful with their cross-platform and multimedia strategy.

Global Citizen Year is a non-profit organization that provides and supports high school graduates with international apprenticeships in social enterprises in developing countries. By facilitating a "bridge year" before college for young adults, Global Citizen Year hopes to better prepare these individuals for university life in the United States—with the ability to speak a second language, a clearer sense of themselves, and a global perspective.

Abby Falik, a Harvard Business School graduate and the founder and CEO of Global Citizen Year, believed that her own experience working with a social enterprise in Nicaragua as a teenager was instrumental in opening her mind. (My own early experiences overseas—strangely enough, in the same rural Nicaraguan village where Falik had lived earlier—had a similar effect on me.) But back when Falik made her sojourn, she had only letters as a way to communicate with friends and family back home. With the advent of widespread Internet and mobile technology, the year-abroad experience has changed in fundamental ways, making current Global Citizen Year fellows more connected than Falik (or I) ever were.

When the first inaugural class of Global Citizen Year fellows headed out into the field in 2009, they immediately began sharing their insights and reflections on the Internet via the Global Citizen Year Fellow's blog. Complete with photos and videos (fellows were given Flip cameras to facilitate new media sharing), these stories brought Global Citizen Year to life.

In their early blog posts, the fellows focused on predeparture excitement or asked people to make a contribution to the Fellows Fund. Posts from their in-country training periods relayed lessons learned from experts in social enterprise and leadership. Soon, their posts transitioned into stories about the fellows meeting the homestay families with whom they would be living for seven months in rural communities across Latin America and Africa.

Similar to the Pepsi Refresh Project (and in contrast to UNICEF), Global Citizen Year *is* a destination website, and their strategy shows how multimedia works well as an integrated part of this setup. Tweeting, for them, is not just a way to extend with new information, but also a way to integrate and bring together the different types of media and the different platforms they were posting on. Videos, blog posts, and pictures could all come together in a short Tweet—with an embedded link to a longer article hosted on the Global Citizen Year blog. Interested followers who clicked through could then easily find more blog posts from the field, more media, as well as official information on the mission of Global Citizen Year and specifics on applying to be a fellow, donating to the organization, or otherwise getting involved.

The fellows at Global Citizen Year provide followers with a unique chance to watch the evolution of an individual through a powerful year in his or her life. From the challenges of learning a new language to the problems facing community farms in Senegal or local entrepreneurs in Guatemala, the GCY fellows' Tweets provide a window into the experiences of high school graduates immersed in a developing nation and the transformation sure to take place over the course of their Global Citizen Year.

8:47 PM Dec 30th, 2010 via TweetDeck

**@GlobalCitizenYr**

"The verb ficar means not only to stay, but to become, and to be" Read Laura Rohrer's post from Brazil - http://bit.ly/hcIHAp #MyResolution

2:13 PM Dec 13th, 2010 via TweetDeck
**@GlobalCitizenYr**

New "day in the life" video from @Nao_Wright,
Fellow stationed at the Millennium Village project in
Leona, Senegal: http://bit.ly/hVtXI3

3:15 PM Dec 1st, 2010 via TweetDeck
**@GlobalCitizenYr**

Fellow @clarasekowski reports from her #health
clinic in Ross Bethio, Senegal. Thoughtful post,
tough situation. http://bit.ly/h189WO

Importantly, the fellows' ability to convey their experience is thanks in huge part to using Twitter via mobile. When we hosted the 2010 fellows at Twitter headquarters before they headed off on their year-long endeavors, this was one of the issues emphasized. Depending on which country they were going to, many of the fellows would be able to tweet via SMS. The others could easily do so with their smart phones. The result proved what it means to be a global citizen. I can be at home (or out and about in San Francisco on my own mobile device), following the updates of these fellows in five countries. Through their photo essays, videos, and blog posts—all collated in simple Tweets—I learn about their daily activities and their changing lives as the year progresses.

Examples of Twitter's use in the field become even more critical in crisis situations, where Tweets can serve as valuable news broadcasts to the world. Twitter allows anyone to be a journalist and an informant to the larger world, and provides a megaphone to amplify the message. In the wake of the Haiti earthquake, Craig Kielburger, founder and CEO of Free the Children, found himself tweeting while he worked with partners on the ground in the days following the earthquake.

His powerful reports from the ground placed him on a short list of the most-followed individuals on the ground in Haiti post-earthquake. The organization has said they owe the rapid growth of this network to social media platforms like Twitter—where their disproportionately young supporters are particularly active. In the next chapter, we'll look at further examples of Twitter's use in the Haiti earthquake—to learn how, as reported in the *New York Times*, "Twitter is transforming the nature of news."

## Social Change in the Field

by Kelly Creeden, director of strategic partnerships
at Free the Children

Throughout history, young people have always been at the forefront of every movement for social change.

Free The Children (FTC) is a by youth, for youth organization founded on the belief that young people have the power to change the world. FTC's model begins in North America, educating young people about local and global issues and empowering them to take action for social change. FTC's programming—which is focused primarily on youth, with a strong emphasis on educators, families, and the corporate world—is built on three guiding principles: Educate, Engage, Empower. Together, these principles work to change attitudes and priorities in North America, helping young people reach out to their friends across the globe through fundraising and awareness campaigns, resulting in sustainable change.

The model then extends to the developing world. The FTC team implements the Adopt a Village program in rural and marginalized areas in Haiti, Kenya, China, India, Sierra Leone, Ecuador, and Sri Lanka. On Twitter, @freethechildren maintains a strong connection to youth around the world by regularly tweeting about project updates and events and promoting their supporters' events and initiatives. FTC's founder, Craig Kielburger (@craigkielburger), uses Twitter to impart a more personal perspective of the work of the organization.

In the wake of a colossal tragedy, this didn't change.

On January 12, 2010, a magnitude 7.0 earthquake struck 15 kilometers from the capital city of Port-au-Prince, devastating the people of Haiti. Two hundred thousand people were feared to be dead and millions more were left homeless. At the time FTC had a ten-year history working in Haiti; they had built nine schools, a nutrition center, and sanitation facilities and helped support teacher salaries and technical training for students. Nearly two thousand children in Haiti attend FTC-funded schools. When the earthquake struck, FTC immediately responded with a strategy focused on protecting children.

A small convoy from FTC, including Craig Kielburger, travelled to Haiti to assist with early response and to carry out rapid needs assessments. During this time, Twitter was crucial for reporting the situation in Haiti back to North America. Because of Twitter, @craigkielburger was able to provide up-to-the-minute, on-the-ground coverage of the earthquake aftermath and relay crucial needs to multiple media outlets. Meanwhile, some news broadcasters had to fight for a single satellite signal available only in Haiti's airport. Thanks to Twitter, @craigkielburger was able to provide young people, other supporters, and the public an immediate opportunity for insight, engagement, and impact. As a result, FTC's early response to Haiti included initial shipments of $1.6 million of emergency supplies and $2 million worth of medical supplies shipped to camps for internally displaced people, hospitals, and strained communities. For the long term, FTC is fully implementing its Adopt a Village model and is committed to getting children quickly and safely back in school and equipping communities to be healthy and sustainable. Young people across North America are fundraising to assist with this effort.

## Connect Your Target with Your Writing Strategy: Crushpad, Twitter, and Finding Your Followers

Throughout the writing process, it is important to ensure that your tweeting stays in line with your Target. The Twitter account for @fledgling—which represents the unique charity endeavor embarked on by Twitter, Room to Read, and Crushpad—gives some insight into what this means.

In the fall of 2009, Room to Read and Twitter launched The Fledgling Initiative together with Crushpad, a local winery that caters to clients who want to make their own wine. After working with some individuals associated with Twitter, Crushpad had proposed a company-wide winemaking endeavor for Twitter. Slowly, the plan began to emerge: Twitter and Room to Read would join together to make a specialty wine created and sold by Crushpad. All proceeds from the sales of the wine would go to Room to Read. The year-long process would be engaging and interesting for the employees at all three organizations and would specifically build bridges between employees at Twitter and employees at Room to Read. Crushpad would serve as the backbone of the operation, making sure things ran smoothly. Along the way, events associated with the project would be a formative part of the experience. During the ten to twelve months of presales—during which period the wine would be available to the public in presales but not yet bottled—employees from Twitter, Room to Read, and Crushpad could take part in a number of winemaking opportunities, including vineyard visits, grape punch-downs, pressings, barrel tasting parties, and bottling events.

The Fledgling Initiative launched in September of 2009 with a simple website cobranded by all three organizations: Twitter, Room to Read, and Crushpad. FledglingWine.com stated its mission: to sell wine for the benefit of Room to Read; every case sold could buy sixty local language books and promote literacy in the world's poorest regions.

The video explaining the initiative started with Twitter cofounder Biz Stone, and the prominent text on the website came from Twitter cofounders. On FledglingWine.com, alongside a passage from John Wood of Room to Read were these official words from cofounders Biz Stone and Evan Williams:

> As a company that's only one percent into its journey, we're always thinking about our long-term impact on the world. The Fledgling Initiative embodies two things that are at the core of Twitter's mission: providing access to information and highlighting the power of open communication to bring about positive change. This initiative is just one piece of that approach. Take part in this mission and pre-buy our limited bottles of the wine. You can follow along with our wine-making activities on Twitter and at some points even participate in its creation. For each bottle you buy, $5 will be donated to Room to Read, a transformational non-profit that brings books, libraries and ultimately literacy to people in the poorest areas around the world. The efforts of Room to Read will benefit literacy, and in doing so they'll allow Twitter to grow. Because if you can't read you can't Tweet!

The Twitter account to go along with it would have to fit the unique partnership and the needs of the accounts' followers. When creating any Twitter account, it's important to remember who the followers are, as the demographic should help inform the nature of the account. For @fledgling, it was understood that the followers would be buyers, employees of all three organizations, and other interested parties. All groups technically fell under the category of potential buyers, so it seemed important that the focus of the account be the wine—with the support of Twitter and Room to Read coming in as secondary elements.

The Target was clear—it needed to be an information account sharing updates about the yearlong process of winemaking, with seasonal focuses on sales and fundraising, as appropriate. The emphasis was placed on the wine, with the idea that buyers would want (mostly) updates about the actual production of the wine itself—with the charity element less emphasized. With this strategy in mind, Crushpad was the best fit to do the majority of the tweeting. Noah Dorrance, former marketing director at Crushpad, explained his rationale for this behind-the-scenes Twitter account talking about the wine's production: "Being involved in the wine industry is kind of the new American dream. By letting people in on each step of the winemaking process through Tweets, photos, and video, we felt we could give followers a portal into the magic of winemaking and something cool to talk about. This made the donation a pleasant bonus to buying a great bottle of wine."

The Fledgling Initiative was an unusual one, and there were multiple players who could have taken the lead with the @fledgling Twitter account. As such, it was important to carefully consider how to best connect the Target of the account with the purpose of the endeavor, ensure that the Writing connected with the Target, and make sure that the Writing best met the needs of the followers.

## A Meditation on Twitter for Global Good

by April Rinne, director of WaterCredit at Water.org and World Economic Forum Young Global Leader

I often find myself viewing the world through a Twitter lens. I go through a day imagining if every aspect of it could be tweeted. Depending on where in the world I wake up that day, I might ask myself: *How long is the wait for a taxi/bus/tuk-tuk to the office/school/store? What's headlining the local news today? Which community kiosk or pump has water this morning? Does the health clinic have its new supply of vaccines yet, so I can take my family there? Are there road blockages, construction or other delays on the roads? Is a particular fruit available at my favorite market, which is far away and I'll only visit if it's there?*

I have used Twitter around the world. I've used it professionally to engage the microfinance community and institutions around the world, increase awareness of the global water and sanitation crisis, and highlight the work of in-country partner organizations. My most memorable experiences related to the power and potential of Twitter as a force for good have come about in travels to far-flung corners of the world. The Twitter lens looks much different in places where web access is scarce, or for a person living at the base of the economic pyramid who can't afford it. This also underscores the massive potential of Twitter via mobiles, which are far cheaper than computers.

My first "Aha!" moment using Twitter came in November 2008, six days after Obama's election as president. I was in rural western Kenya and given the surprise opportunity to meet his grandmother Sarah. Because Kenya didn't have a Twitter short code at the time (and I didn't have a smart phone with me in the field), I texted a friend in the United States who tweeted my news by proxy. Later, having retweeted that from the nearest village Internet connection, I discovered scores of new followers: people near and far had somehow found me and thought that what I had to say was worthwhile.

Since then I've had many other poignant experiences revealing both the utility of Twitter and the limitations where it does not exist. In the Himalaya, without mobile or internet access, I resorted to taking photos of the Tweets I wanted to send and then reposting them several days later.

For individuals and organizations in the developing world, there are myriad practical uses for Twitter that don't necessarily exist elsewhere. For example, it is estimated that worldwide, two hundred million hours are spent *each day* collecting water, and up to 25 percent of a poor family's income may be used to purchase water. Imagine if it were possible to target, track—and tweet—the availability and price of water in urban slums? And how easy would it be to couple that with helpful information about sanitation and hygiene? Or imagine if successful microfinance platforms like @kiva were deployed at the grassroots level and Kiva clients could Tweet among themselves and with the broader community. A farmer who'd taken a loan for seeds could get information about weather, a fisherman who'd taken a loan for a net could get information about the market price for fish, a tailor who'd saved up for a sewing machine could get information about fabrics, and all of them could get information about financial management and planning.

Twitter's value is profound on multiple levels: individual, organizational, transactional, governmental, societal, and more. For non-profit and cause-based organizations, its utility is broad and its impacts—whether focused on fundraising, information-sharing, or reputation and visibility—can be nothing short of phenomenal.

At the same time, however, a lingering question remains in my mind: How do we bridge the gap between non-profits and social enterprises' use of Twitter "at home" and use by the people and communities around the world that they serve? One key link in doing this is SMS.

SMS is ubiquitous in the developing world. Poor and more affluent people alike understand the power of texting and employ it constantly. Mobile penetration rates certainly help this; indeed, there are more cell phones than toilets in India (a sad comment on sanitation there, but that's another topic). While SMS offers principally one-on-one communications, Twitter's "follow" design makes it much better suited to disseminating information. Fulfilling Twitter's original SMS vision with a global footprint would likely bring great benefits worldwide.

## Top Questions on the "Write" Step

Q: Who should write the Tweets?

A: Finding the right person to do your tweeting is an important part of making sure your strategy on Twitter works, for both your organization and your followers. As discussed in Chapter Two, it is essential that the person in charge of tweeting (say, your social media manager) be a part of the process of deciding what Target your account should have.

In more complex cause campaign initiatives that bring together multiple interests (like The Fledgling Initiative), thinking about the expectations and needs of the followers can help in deciding who should be in charge of the Writing so that it best ties in with the overall campaign Target.

The topic of who does the tweeting is top of mind for celebrities and other high-profile individuals who often outsource their tweeting. After Conan O'Brien was famously fired from NBC's *The Tonight Show*, he kept in touch with his fans (who were used to seeing him every night on television) by joining Twitter. Quickly, @conanobrien created a storm on the service by creating one stellar, hysterical Tweet a day, and making headlines by following only one individual. As such, it should perhaps be no surprise that when he came to

Twitter headquarters in San Francisco in April of 2010 he said that he did all his own tweeting (with the help of his team, who make sure he's actually funny).

Ryan Seacrest professed a similar stance when he visited Twitter headquarters in November of 2010, the same week he launched the Ryan Seacrest Foundation to enhance the lives of seriously ill and injured children. He proudly—and emphatically—told us that he wrote his own Tweets. When asked about his opinions of other celebrities who did pass off their tweeting duties to others, he responded that it was definitely something you have to be careful about—because followers want your voice. The question is a sticky one. "For the first time in history, any individual has the power to broadcast out to an audience, without having to go through a media company," explained Omid Ashtari, in business development at Twitter focusing on media and entertainment. "More importantly, it's an audience willing to listen, as they opt-in to get information from each person or company. Many high-profile individuals have figured this out and take great advantage of the power of Twitter, whether for their own personal gain or to aid in their philanthropic missions. The audience is savvy, and users who are not authentic are drowned out and their audience stops listening."

## Who Should Do the Tweeting at Your Organization?

By John Carnell, CEO of BullyingUK

Thanks to Twitter and the power of its users to spread messages and tell each other about cool things they encounter, hundreds of thousands of people now know about our anti-bullying work at BullyingUK. Twitter has allowed us to put a voice and personality behind our organization's brand. As CEO I feel it's my duty to tweet. We have volunteers helping out on some of our other Twitter accounts, but I think to get our message across to the general public it needs to come from the very top of the organization. Where else is the heart and soul of the organization than at the point where the decisions happen?

For best results, Twitter should be used by a person who has the power and authority to make decisions. Twitter users expect a reply within fifteen minutes if they can see you're online (you sent out a Tweet recently); if you fail to reply or give some excuse about needing to get advice from a higher-up, then you have really lost the magic of Twitter—the ability to very quickly respond and react to the general public on their terms, not ours. My advice would be, if the CEO won't or can't tweet, then it should be a senior PR person or someone from the volunteer coordination team. It must be someone with experience of the general public and who has a clear passion for the subject matter. If all else fails and it has to be given to a junior member of the team, then that person should have the full backing of the organization. They are, after all, *your voice* on Twitter. You gave them the power, so you can't blame them if they mess it up on your behalf.

Q: Who should *send* the Tweets?

A: Although you might think this is the same question as "Who Should Write the Tweets?" it's definitely not! I often get asked whether someone else can or should send the Tweets on behalf of the account's "voice."

When I worked with Sean Penn's staff to explore onboarding his organization, J/P Haitian Relief Organization, one solution they suggested—and that works well—is to have a trusted advisor who regularly travels with the celebrity do the tweeting, and have the "voice" sign off. I would argue, though, that this is not necessary. If you're on your phone, or connected to the Internet, you can use Twitter. It really is that easy.

If you are convinced that you need to hire someone, however, Chapter Six provides tips about how to make sure they are in tune with the strategy your organization sets for itself on Twitter.

Q:  How often should I tweet?

A:  We all love directions on exactly how to excel, and talking about how often to Tweet is a favorite—and highly contested—question I hear in trainings and workshops. I did a random survey of Twitter employees and Twitter aficionados to see what they thought. This is what they said:

@**tiger:** I Tweet rather a lot at times.

@**neongolden:** I follow Biz's suggestions of "as often as you eat," and try to limit it to 3x daily.

@**sacca:** I try to not set any firm schedule or any frequency goals as I think that would dilute my Tweets. Sometimes, there is nothing to be said. Other times, I can't help but share my ideas, reactions, hopes, and curiosity with my followers. When

I Tweet, I am asking my followers for their most scarce resource—their attention. I want to deliver something of value.

**@kanter:** When I have something of value to my network that can help them change the world by doing a better job of effectively using Twitter to support their mission.

**@johnwoodRTR:** 2–3 times per day.

**@charitywater** and **@scottharrison:** We tweet 1–5 times a day. Every day we post a "pic of the day," and we regularly share news and RT supporters.

**@jennadawn:** Once a day unless I'm traveling or in a conversation.

**@troy:** 5–10 per day from @calibersf; 3–5 per week from @jpeg (my dog); 3 per month from @herbcaen; as necessary from @support; and every Twitter/support Tweet gets RT from my admin @tholden.

**@briggles:** Once a day.

**@nancybroden:** I tweet at certain times of the day—morning (at breakfast), afternoon (lunch) and in the evening, generally while watching TV and just before bed. In each session I generally produce 1–2 original Tweets, and retweet about 5–8 Tweets by others.

**@shinypb:** Whenever I'm overcome by the beauty, wonderfulness, ridiculousness, or frustration of a situation.

**@netik:** I tweet once or twice a day, but if I'm at a conference or music event, I'll tweet once or twice an hour to coordinate conference events and to meet people.

**@delbius:** Varies depending on the number of people asking me questions on a given day, but non @-replies are 1–7 per day generally, with the bell curve being around 1–4.

**@sprsquish:** I average out to a few times an hour.

**@jess:** A few times a day.

**@thx4beinawesome:** Once per quarter.

**@danadanger:** 1–3 times per day, not counting @replies.

**@mischa:** I try to stay around 8 to 10 times a day.

Although there is no one answer, and it varies dramatically depending on what you're tweeting about, suffice it to say that tweeting more than @thx4beingawesome (who Tweets once a quarter) would be a good idea;)

Q: Can I delete a Tweet?

   A: Your mother might say that the proper question here is not "Can I delete a Tweet?," but rather "May I delete a Tweet?" Indeed, functionality clearly allows for Tweet deletion, but is this a good idea? Does it even help, given that many people will have already seen the Tweet you now want to delete?

Although deleting is not ideal, I do it on occasion. Particularly when I notice a spelling error or inadvertently send a Tweet before completing it, I find that immediately reposting a "better" version of one Tweet after deleting the original is fine. People who already saw the first one likely already got the message (despite your spelling errors or lack of punctuation), and posterity will now see that you *can* spell and that you *did* have a fully formed Tweet in your mind when writing.

3 Mar via HootSuite

**@ClaireD**

I admit. I did a Tweet deletion last night. Only happens a few times a year. #tweetfail

http://twitter.com/#!/ClaireD/status/43327597098176512

Q: Should I geotag my Tweets?

A: Many individuals have their Twitter accounts set to show the location from which they send each Tweet. This can be extremely interesting—and useful. Should an organization show their geolocation status to their followers in their Tweets? The question really depends on the amount of travel involved in the account holder's tweeting.

Take John Wood's personal account, @johnwoodrtr, and the Room to Read main account, @roomtoread, as two examples. Given that John Wood travels two-thirds of the year to interesting places all over the globe, reading his locations adds an element of added interest to his Tweets. He tweets about his runs at least once a week, and the simple addition of a geolocation tag can turn what seems like "yet another" Tweet about John's weekly jogging efforts into something fresh. *Today he's jogging in Bangalore? But he was just running in South Africa just a few days ago!* Similarly, I've always been fascinated by Jane Goodall, whose Jane Goodall Institute tweets from @janegoodallinst. At seventy-six, she still spends three hundred days a year travelling the world. She, for one, would be aided immensely by geolocation.

In contrast, Room to Read's organizational account, @roomtoread, is run by Rebecca Hankin, director of communications and marketing. Rebecca spends most of her year in San Francisco, so if she had her account set to include geolocation in her Tweets, it wouldn't be terribly interesting to readers. Worst than that, it could become boring.

Q: Should I send automatic feeds for picture, video, or blog posts to Twitter? If I do send automatic RSS feeds, should I do so on all my social networks or just one?

A: You should definitely be alerting your readers on all your social media platforms about new content at your dynamic website, and doing so via an automatic RSS or through manual updates works fine. Keep in mind that if you do choose to do so through automatic RSS, you should ensure that your headlines are not the same on all your networks. For instance, if you have a new blog post called "A Day of Learning in Brazil's Favelas," you don't want the exact Tweet or Facebook status update duplicated with the same words in all the venues where your RSS is sent automatically.

Also consider that open rates and click-through rates may be different depending on whether the update is sent automatically or manually posted, and you'll want to compare the results. Play with this until you find the right balance: making sure your readers are getting all the new updates without wearing yourself out by constantly sending out manual updates.

For more tips on integrating Twitter with your organizational blogging efforts, see http://twitter4good.com/resources/blogging/

**WEB**

# E (Engage): Tools to Win

Twitter allows you the chance to reach a wider audience than ever before. But unless you're Kanye, that vast audience might not take notice the minute you start tweeting. To get your writing noticed, you need to *Engage*.

At first, this can seem overwhelming. The key is in learning how to get your words in front of users who care. Connecting your Tweets with existing relevant information that people are already viewing on Twitter—or making your own Tweets the relevant information that others are looking for—should be your goal. The Twitter platform allows a variety of built-in functionalities to help you reach this aim. In this chapter, we'll look at exactly how to do so to best Engage on Twitter.

## Built-in Functionality You Should Be Using

### #Hashtags

For those new to Twitter, hashtags are a way to add further context to your Tweets. Simply put a hash symbol (#) in your Tweet, followed by a keyword, topic, or theme that each particular Tweet addresses. This will help identify your Tweet as part of a group of like-minded Tweets, and those following lists of particular hashtags will be able to find your Tweets more easily.

Hashtags are a fantastic way for organizations to build movements. Nike's Laura Adams, who leads Global Sustainable Business & Innovation Digital for the company, agrees. She believes that Nike's Better World Campaign on Twitter has been aided through hashtags. "Nike's used the #nikebetterworld hashtag to unite the conversation and energy around Nike Better World." In effect, "the hashtag has helped us tie together the different facets of Better World around Nike's belief in and commitment to building a better world through sport and leveraging unlikely collaborations to unleash innovation. In the future, we see Twitter and hashtags playing an even bigger role in helping our consumers engage in Better World. They are a valuable way to generate awareness and energy at a mass scale." Indeed, getting people behind your hashtag is key, and if done with great success, your hashtag can even "trend" on Twitter (multiple tweets with the same hashtag form trends, and very popular trends can get lots of exposure), getting in front of many more people than you might have first envisioned. In 2009, the thousands of attendees actively tweeting at the

Skoll World Forum for Social Entrepreneurship in Oxford, England, were able to get their hashtag trending by doing just that:

27 Mar 09 via mobile web

**@SkollWorldForum**

Skoll World Forum is the 6th most twitted topic right now on Twitter. Thanks for the interaction! #swf09

http://twitter.com/#!/SkollWorldForum/status/1400914939

John Carnell, CEO of Bullying UK, claims that his favorite endeavor to date on Twitter has been making the hashtag #charitytuesday an active part of the Twitter sphere. He says, "I spotted the tag one Tuesday morning floating past my stream and thought—what a great way to allow the general public to say thanks or recommend charities. I then used the power of our network to get the word out about it; for the first three weeks we had a trending topic and now people from all over the world use it to promote organizations they care about. I think it's had a huge impact on charities' use of Twitter, and I know of a number of non-profit organizations that have joined Twitter just to take part in #charitytuesday."

Hashtags are a fantastic way to join an existing conversation already targeted to a topic of interest—or to create your own. Although I spent years creating hashtags that never caught on (read #nyquildreams and #akenyanmosquitojustdiedonmyface), in March of 2011 I was happy to lead a social innovation workshop at South by Southwest that resulted in a very relevant hashtag: #Twitter4Good.

7  seconds ago via web

**@ClaireD**

It's the hashtag you've been waiting for.
#Twitter4Good

http://twitter.com/#!/ClaireD/status/51838145725079553

Events are a hugely popular time for hashtag creation—and if your organization is participating in a conference (or is unable to attend but wishes you were), using the correct hashtag will get your thoughts in front of people who care about your issue. Samasource, an organization that seeks to bring jobs to the world's poorest, is one organization that uses hashtags effectively. Samasource's motto is "Give Work," and this social enterprise works hard to bring dignified, computer-based work to women, youth, and refugees living in poverty. From refugees in Kenya to women in rural Pakistan, the populations served use Samasource to find life-changing work opportunities via the Internet. In parallel, Samasource enables socially responsible companies, small businesses, nonprofits, and entrepreneurs in the United States to contribute to economic development by buying services from their workforce at fair prices. At Samasource they are constantly working to spread the message about their work to find new donors and supporters, and conferences are one venue in which to do so. With Twitter, they've been able to tap into a way to make the speaking events they attend have even more impact—by reaching those at home as well.

Leila Janah, founder and CEO of Samasource, explained,

We attend dozens of conferences and speaking engagements each year on subjects like poverty, outsourcing, and

development. Twitter enables us to have many members
of our organization interacting with people in an audience instead of just our main speaker. It moves a topic like
Crowdsourcing for Good from just a question-and-answer
format panel discussion to an ongoing event that people
can participate in by using [a hashtag]. While one member
of our organization is answering questions on the panel,
several more can be using Twitter to spread the answers and
to respond to follow up questions online.

Hashtags are certainly not just for time-sensitive events,
however; there are many hashtags that run every day, year
in and year out, like #charitytuesday and #followfriday
(a hashtag encouraging you to find and follow new users
every Friday). Following these hashtags to see what people
are saying about your cause on any given day keeps you
informed of recent events and key players in the field on
Twitter. When you contribute Tweets to that particular
stream by using that hashtag, you establish yourself as a
voice on the topic as well. Third-party Twitter clients like
Hootsuite can also create ready-made streams of hashtags so
that you can constantly follow an increasingly long list of
hashtags relevant to your cause.

It's important to always be relevant when using your
hashtags. Some Twitter users get into the habit of tack-
ing on hashtags even when a particular Tweet is not
related; this is surely one of the easiest ways to get individuals who would otherwise be interested in your cause to
deem you a spammer, ignore your Tweets, or even unfol-
low you. Additionally, don't stick any and every hashtag
you know of that *might* be relevant to a Tweet you are
proud of.

Organizations on Twitter could learn a thing or two from hashtag extraordinaire Carrie Isaac, founder of ColoradoBargains.com, whose mission is to help Colorado families save money on the things they have to buy. She says, "I see a lot of people tweeting something they want lots of people to see, so they stick two or three or four (or more—*shudder*) hashtags on the Tweet to increase its visibility."

19 Dec via Twitter for iPhone

    **@carriei**

In most cases, using more than one hashtag in your tweets makes you look like a spammer.

http://twitter.com/carriei/status/16532772822712322#

As Isaac explains, there are a few key problems with this practice. "One, the content of the Tweet is lost in the clutter of the hashtags. You can't see the Tweet because of the hashtags. Two, people immediately recognize that you used those hashtags in order to gain visibility from people that may not be following you."

11 Mar

**@carriei**

Look at your tweets on Twitter.com when you use a lot of hashtags. All the hashtags are in blue, and they look REALLY spammy. #justsayin

http://twitter.com/carriei/status/46357981121609728#

Given the purpose of the hashtag, Isaac emphasizes how overuse of hashtags is spam at it worst. "You want to be relevant in the hashtags that you use, and make sure you understand the context of those hashtags so you're not mistaken as spamming. If you don't participate in a hashtag and aren't part of that hashtag community, you may not understand its purpose, audience, or subject matter—and if you use it for a purpose that's outside the scope of that hashtag community you may [gain an unfortunate] reputation in that community for tweeting irrelevant or even offensive content."

Newbie users are especially adept at using too many hashtags.

When @sammyikua and I first met at Tumaini Children's Home in Kenya many years ago, I learned right away he was ace at technology. After he had spent just a few hours a week on the orphanage computer during his preteens, he was able to fix any computer woe I could come up with. These days, Twitter is just one more tool this connected teen uses to talk with the world about global citizenship (his favorite topic, as a trilingual Kenyan finishing high school in the United States). But his overeagerness can sometimes be a bad thing, as in this Tweet:

28 March via TweetDeck

**@sammyikua**

How many of you know the millenium goals? http://on.fb.me/hahgfa get them! #twitter4good #citizenship #world #international #global @ClaireD

http://twitter.com/#!/sammyikua/status/52212624397582336

Although I applauded his use of my new hashtag #Twitter4Good, I'm sure I wasn't the only one who thought his otherwise valuable article link got lost in the glare of too many hashtags. As Sammy's guardian, I had no qualms setting his Tweet straight:

28 Mar via HootSuite

**@ClaireD**

@sammyikua ok i retweeted but try to use no more than 2 hashtags on any tweet (unless you're making a joke) bc it looks spammy

http://twitter.com/#!/ClaireD/status/52234404550025216

Aside from overtagging, you should also avoid using overly general words as hashtags. Using the incredibly broad hashtags #world and #international (as @sammyikua did above) won't get your Tweets in front of interested parties, and it will make you look like a spammer, a newbie, or both. The best hashtags are specific phrases that, ideally, others are also using.

The country of Argentina is wild for Twitter, and one of the nation's top newspapers even has an online section devoted to Twitter news (see http://140.perfil.com/). Argentina in particular has set itself apart on the platform by the sheer number of uncannily active politicians. The powerful minister of foreign relations for the country, Héctor Timerman, is even known as "Twitterman." As such, it was no surprise that Argentines began using hashtags wildly in the lead-up to the 2011 Argentine presidential elections. Amazingly, some politicians (and banners throughout the city) showed that even extremely long hashtags like #EchemosLuzSobreMacri could work if the users were passionate.

The message is clear: to create or join a conversation, use carefully chosen hashtags prolifically, but only when relevant. After all, your hashtag can reach farther than you expected, and can even spark a movement. @alya1989262 is a twenty-one-year-old Egyptian student who was the first to send a Tweet with the #Jan25 hashtag during the January 2011 Egyptian Revolution. During one of the most important moments in her country's recent history, she coined a Twitter hashtag that symbolized the movement—online and off.

## #Jan25
### by @alya1989262

I'm almost 22. I've lived in Egypt since I was 5 (spent the years before that in France). I signed up for Twitter I think 2 years ago or so, but only started using it intensively in the past 7 or 8 months.

Twitter is a very important tool for protesters, as evidenced by the fact that it and Facebook were repeatedly blocked in Egypt as the protests flared up. We use it to campaign and spread the word about protests/stands—hashtags are invaluable in that respect, and to share news quickly and efficiently, with our own 140-char commentary on them, and subsequently have conversations with random people/complete strangers. But most importantly, it allows us to share on the ground info like police brutality, things to watch out for, activists getting arrested, etc. A certain class of activists are armed with smartphones, which allow them to live-Tweet the protests (for example, some people Tweet the chants, because they're often funny and interesting). When it comes to organisation, I think Facebook is the main new media tool there. Twitter trends also help us gauge how visible we are to the international community (my trends feed is set to Worldwide, and I know a lot of people have it set to various places in the US). Making our voices heard, making sure people outside Egypt are aware of what's going on is very important to us, especially with the recent cell lines and internet blackout last weekend.

One more thing is that the government has recently been trying to make use of social media—in a painfully awkward (but not surprising) manner. I've seen several Twitter accounts with few Tweets and no more than 5 followers/following, tweeting about how bad the protests are for the stability of the country, how great the president is, etc. It's always the same few Tweets, with the same wording, over several accounts. But most of the government's propaganda is done over state TV, which is unfortunately far more convincing to the average Egyptian citizen than a bunch of young people on the Internet. But right now, we're planning how to use social media to counter government propaganda that paints protesters as violent, confused youth, misled by "foreign elements" into harming our own country. We need to enter the conversation with people who believe what they're told on TV, and the best way to do that is using social media to present our arguments in a calm, logical manner.

For years, the ruling party portrayed the political scene in Egypt as a struggle between themselves, the secular National Democratic Party, and the Muslim Brotherhood, with the Egyptian left wing completely marginalised for lack of inspirational leaders. We, the non-Brotherhood opposition, were left waiting for a magical spiritual leader a la Obama, who would inspire us to revolt against the NDP. Tunisia showed us that a popular revolution can take place and topple a dictatorial regime, without the need for strong leadership and tight organisation. January 14 was the day we started believing in January 25.

Tying this back to Twitter, the Tunisian revolution was barely covered by traditional media until Ben Ali fled, but the #tunisia and #sidibouzid hashtags allowed us to follow the events for the whole month beforehand. I think that further convinced us of the power each of us has to effect change.

Source: http://hope140.org/blog/.

**WEB**   See a list of some great hashtags to follow at http://twitter4good.com/resources/hashtags/

## Use Lists

Every Twitter user should be using lists. They are a great way to find relevant accounts and information and position yourself well in front of those interested in your cause. Lists aren't static directories of Twitter handles, but rather living Twitter streams from individuals you choose. Not only can you use lists to organize the people you follow into relevant groups, but you can also follow the relevant Tweets of people on lists—even if you aren't following those individuals. Find lists on the top right-hand side of your timeline, and use them with abandon. Here are a few different ways to make the best use of lists:

***Search and Follow Lists:*** Searching for lists is a fantastic way to find individuals who are consistently tweeting about themes you are also interested in. Christie George is the director of New Media Ventures, the first national network of early stage investors in start-ups focused on building progressive change. She is constantly searching for relevant information to help her investors, and lists are one way to do this. "I've found lists most helpful when I need to get caught up on a topic quickly—especially one that may only be of momentary importance. I find someone whose voice I appreciate, whose network seems interesting, and can check out a relevant list without drowning out the friends and colleagues that I'd like to hear from more regularly."

As opposed to hashtags, lists allow you to follow all the Tweets of an individual within your interest graph—not just the Tweets they have denoted with relevant hashtags. In the long run, this is an important step in helping you develop relationships with these users. Although at first it may seem unnecessary to read the personal Tweets of a potential organizational supporter or donor, it is important to remember that learning about people's personal lives and connecting with them on these themes is the best way to build the relationships that ultimately lead to professional collaboration. George explains, "I like how institutions have used lists as a way of promoting the personal voices of their staff (for example, @neworganizing). Even when I know that individuals are speaking for themselves (and not on behalf of their organizations), it really helps to get a sense of the people that power the mission."

*Create Your Own Lists:*   If you can't find a list that exactly targets your demographic or interest group, the best thing to do is to make your own. People on Twitter love when others place them on lists, and when they find out that you've placed them on your list, they are likely to check out your account, the list in question, and the other users involved.

Creating your own lists is another way to make better or more targeted lists than already exist. For example, let's say you are a New York City–based foundation aiming to meet and connect with other foundations doing similar work. Although you have already searched for (and found) a great list of like-minded foundations all over the world, you realize that the list in question is simply too broad for you; you want to be able to find executives in philanthropy in your community. Solve the problem by simply creating your own list of NYC-based foundations to help narrow down the players.

When creating a list, make sure you're not the only person on it. From the get-go, you want to add key players in the field, both large and small—remembering that large or high-profile organizations may increase the lists' credibility, but smaller organizations may be more likely to actively engage.

The National Park Foundation is one example of an organization using lists on a daily basis, and to aid in times of crisis. Chartered by Congress in 1967, the National Park Foundation is the official charity of America's national parks and was established to strengthen the connection between the American people and their parks to aid in preservation. When the Deepwater Horizon oil spill disaster in the Gulf of Mexico occurred in 2010, the National Park Foundation focused on steering volunteers and donors to make an immediate impact. Trevor Martin, the manager of new media, described how the Foundation had created lists on Twitter prior to the spill to maintain relationships with many national parks units and provide relevant National Park Foundation information on grants, programs, and partnerships. In the midst of disaster, Martin says, "These lists helped the foundation stay on top of information relevant to the parks and give minute-by-minute details about what was going on in those national parks most impacted by the Gulf oil spill."

***Private Versus Public Lists:*** Although most of the list suggestions so far have to do with making sure others see the lists you are making and taking part in, private lists are also an important tool for causes to use. Organizations need to stay top of mind for relevant journalists and public relations representatives, and a great way to do so is to create private lists where you follow the individuals you eventually want to pitch something to. No one else needs to see these lists, and you can keep these private, viewable only by you. With a private list like this, you can regularly keep track of certain individuals and send them an @reply (or even a direct message, if they are following you) when they send out a relevant Tweet. Building a relationship over Twitter is a great stepping-stone to further professional efforts down the line; we'll talk more about this in the next chapter.

## Use @reply …

Don't tweet in a bubble. Not only is it boring, but it won't get your organization where you need to be. Engaging is all about bringing others into the conversation when they otherwise might not have found their own way in. One easy way to do this is to mention others in your Tweets via an @reply. People watch who @replies them, and using @replies smartly can put you on their radar. Like the hashtag, the @reply is a user-generated feature created when frequent Twitter users found a need for it. The key with the @reply is to make sure you're using it, and to make sure you're using it well.

For many organizations, the @reply is the perfect way to engage in real-time customer service. Tara Roth McConaghy, the former COO of GOOD, Inc., and the senior advisor on the Pepsi Refresh Project, says that Twitter's power for the Pepsi Refresh Project was about more than its ability to bring awareness to the campaign. It also allowed for real-time support for participants. She says, "Not only was Twitter an effective tool for campaigners to promote their particular cause, but it also provided a corporate communications outlet for companies like Pepsi and GOOD to answer technical questions about how to submit projects—establishing a one-to-one, dynamic relationship with customers and consumers, while also affording other Twitter followers the benefit of that information."

If you are on the side of the individual trying to engage with potential sponsors and supporters, mentioning them via @reply is a great way to stay top of mind. Following an important meeting, think of sending an @reply as a way to remind a potential collaborator of your key message. As an example, Global Citizen Year once had a promising meeting with the SunPower Foundation about how the foundation might best help Global Citizen Year fellows find global apprenticeships in the solar space. To firm up the connection, and formalize their ask for support, Global Citizen Year sent out a Tweet after the meeting as a quick summary:

22 Jan via TweetDeck

**@GlobalCitizenYr**

Great meeting w/@SunPeople about how we can get our Fellows involved with solar around the world. Very exciting to be getting into energy!

http://twitter.com/#!/GlobalCitizenYr/status/8091078743

The Tweet served two purposes. Not only did it tell @globalcitizenyr followers what Global Citizen Year was up to, but it also reminded the SunPower Foundation about the meeting and the importance it held for Global Citizen Year.

Indeed, the public nature of an @reply is important, and there's a reason people send @replies when they could send direct messages.

The @reply helps create accountability. Because anyone can see the @replies directed toward you, one could argue that a potential collaborator is more likely to respond to an @reply than an email. It's an intuitive way to ask something in a public way, and it was actually created organically by Twitter users.

In 2007—before I knew how to use @replies correctly—I tweeted from Kenya hoping to catch the attention of the race directors of the Lewa Wildlife Conservancy Safaricom Marathon, where I was taking a bunch of teens from the orphanage where I lived on behalf of my non-profit organization.

9 Apr 07 via im

**@ClaireD**

How can we get the Safaricom marathon in Kenya to waive the entrance fees for the kids??? Same question as always...

http://twitter.com/#!/ClaireD/status/22878211

Without my using an @reply mentioning Safaricom's Twitter handle (if they even had one in 2007), the chances of Safaricom finding the Tweet was low. Years later, I've changed my approach. In 2010, I gave a talk at a conference where Procter & Gamble, maker of Gain laundry detergent, was offering free robes to speakers. Annoyed that I forgot to pick up my (free! freshly laundered!) robe, I tweeted about my anguish to some other speakers, putting @alliworthington, the cofounder of Blissdom Conferences, on the Tweet. Not only did she reply to my @reply and send me a robe, but she also (miraculously) still became my friend.

## . . . But Avoid @reply Spam

As always, the important thing about the @reply is to use it responsibly—which is to say, make sure that what you are writing is relevant to the entity you are tagging. The latter half of 2010 saw the rise of Paper.li, an application that "organizes links shared on Twitter and Facebook into an easy-to-read newspaper-style format"—and with it the (sad) rise of irrelevant @replies. It was frustrating to see individuals I otherwise think of as quality Twitter users using my username (@ClaireD) irrelevantly in these updates, and in late 2010 the situation had gotten so out of hand that many began a concerted effort to subscribe out of paper.li @reply spam. It was a wonderful morning when I woke up and saw the following Tweet from @biz recommending just how to do so using an original opt-out account called @newscrier:

2:34 PM Nov 6th via Tweet Button

**@biz**

@NewsCrier please stop mentions
http://t.co/Ef8J2p9

http://twitter.com/biz/status/964191473115137

Within minutes, my @reply stream was much cleaner.

## Retweet!

One of the easiest ways to engage on Twitter is to retweet. People love seeing their words repeated and passed on, and many Twitter users take great pride in tracking the number of retweets a given Tweet earned and the "distance" the

Tweet traveled. (Think of it as a bit like a six degrees of separation game, inspired by Twitter.)

It's important not to become too overzealous in retweeting, however. If one follower retweets every Tweet your organization writes, their recommendation for you holds less weight. Take this to the extreme and you'll find many an account set up by a spammer whose sole purpose is to automatically retweet highly followed accounts.

With retweets, you also want to make sure that you don't fall into the trap of becoming a lazy Twitter user. Especially on a busy day or week, it can be very tempting to forget about writing your own Tweets and to simply retweet what others are saying. This is particularly true when you are good at Engaging and you find yourself constantly exposed to high-quality content via lists and hashtags you follow. As an example, I manage Twitter's @hope140 account, Twitter's account that focuses on being a force for good. There are clearly many examples in the Twittersphere of Twitter's use in humanitarian or prosocial causes, and I constantly receive great tales of non-profits using Twitter via lists I follow, hashtags, or @replies. As a result, I am often tempted to retweet a bit too often. After all, how important is it to simply rewrite a Tweet that you saw somewhere else in your own words, instead of just retweeting it? It turns out it can be quite important, as too many retweets in your timeline tell your followers that you aren't developing your own quality content. You *can* have too much of a good thing. A timeline full to the brim with retweets just may send the message that you can't come up with anything good enough on your own to say.

## Ask Questions

Asking questions is one of the best ways to Engage with Twitter. Indeed, one of the first things I ask organizations who want to improve their use of Twitter is whether they are asking enough questions of their followers. Creating a weekly question related to your mission is a great way to instantly up engagement. When in doubt, go for questions that offer people the chance to say their opinion, and not to answer with a "right" or "wrong" answer. When it's a personal question, everyone can offer an answer via an @reply.

See a list of some of the best questions to ask your Twitter followers at http://twitter4good.com/resources/best-questions/  **WEB**

## Promote Products on Twitter

Finally, no discussion of tools is complete without a nod to the paid and pro bono products Twitter offers to advertise your organization or cause. There are a range of paid promoted products on Twitter that fit every brand—for-profit or non-profit.

For non-profits interested in pro bono advertising, we also offer several options. Pro-Bono Promoted Tweets for Good and Pro-Bono Crisis Tweets are application-based programs that take on select numbers of (registered 501[c][3]) non-profits each year. As the name suggests, Pro-Bono Crisis Tweets are devoted to non-profit organizations responding in times of crisis. Although the wait list is long for the pro bono programs, the opportunity is a great (free) one for causes; find more information at www.Hope140.org.

Although the specific programs will change over time, the concept remains—promoted products offer ways for organizations to better reach interested parties on the Twitter platform and to benefit from innovative, creative ideas that answer people's current needs. In the aftermath of the catastrophic 2011 Japan earthquake and tsunami, for example, some paid advertisers took up this challenge. Realizing they could best serve the public by nixing their current campaign and instead providing useful tsunami-related information, regardless of its connection to their brand, they changed up their advertising on the fly. For example, BuzzFeed, a technology website, started running this promoted Tweet:

**@Results for #tsunami**

**60 NEW TWEETS**                                22 minutes ago
**BuzzFeed**

Here are some practical ways you can help earthquake and tsunami victims in Japan now: http://goo.gl/ooEVJ #tsunami

Whether coming from a paid client (like @BuzzFeed) or a pro bono client (like @HawaiiRedCross), these types of promoted Tweets did exactly what good advertising should do—addressed people's real-time needs:

about 3 hours ago via web

**@HawaiiRedCross**

There are several resources available at http://newsroom.redcross.org/ to check up on loved ones that may have been affected by #tsunami

Let's now explore more deeply just how to use these tools to stand out.

## Connect Others with Resources

As many of the built-in engagement tools on Twitter reveal, the real beauty of Twitter lies in the fact that it is not a one-to-one service, but rather a one-to-many service—allowing you to both follow and learn from all the many individuals who do not personally follow you. When people ask me "What's the first thing I should do when I sign up for Twitter?" I say "Help someone." It's true. There is no better way to get noticed than to directly meet someone else's need. I have seen few individuals on Twitter who do this better than Mark Horvath.

Mark is the founder of InvisiblePeople.tv, but he prefers to brand himself as Invisible People's Chief Evangelistic Officer, Do-Gooder, and Loudmouth. Every day, Horvath works hard to connect homeless people with resources. Horvath used to be homeless himself, and he intimately understands the population. Specifically, he knows the nature of Internet use among homeless people. As he explained when he came to talk with us at Twitter headquarters, homeless populations in the United States spend immense amounts of time on computers in public libraries.

On his blog, Horvath described—in Tweets—how Twitter helped one family over the Christmas holidays. Horvath had met a woman at a shelter who was living in her van with her nine-year-old son. When the city towed the van, the family had lost everything. Horvath had stepped in to check them into a hotel and take them grocery shopping. When the mother said she desperately needed a change of clothes—and another women at the shelter chimed in—Horvath broadcast the needs via his Twitter account, @hardlynormal.

You about 17 hours ago from Tweetie

ANOTHER mom w/ 9yo boy has nothing! She needs clothes and the boy needs clothes! They are living in their van which was towed! HELP?

URGENT! homeless woman needs clothes. Health issues she's peed in same pants 3 days. 4x-5x pants/shirts sz 12 undies. needs socks! HELP?

Almost instantly, Pastor Matthew Barnett of the Los Angeles Dream Center sent Horvath the following direct message via Twitter:

about 17 hours ago

**@MatthewBarnett**

I'm in. How much cash you need. I'm all over it!

about 17 hours ago

**@MatthewBarnett**

I can drop it off tnite. Take him shopping at mall tomm?

Horvath described what happened next:

Because the only clothes this mother and child had were on their backs, I didn't feel we could wait another day. I searched the GPS on my phone and the closest store was Walmart. I tweeted that I was headed there. Soon, Pastor Matthew called me and asked me to pick out a nice toy for the boy and suggested a Nintendo DS. The Los Angeles Dream Center is the church that helped me off the streets, and Matthew Barnett has been caring for homeless people for over a decade. He knows people without housing cannot carry lots of stuff, so a portable video game is a perfect gift.

I'm holding back tears! **@matthewbarnett** is on his way to meet us at walmart to bless this family! Oh crap, too late can't hold em back :)

The family is shopping for clothes. **@matthewbarnett** asked us to pick out a NICE toy for boy, family doesn't know ! Gonna be a WOW night :)

**@hardlynormal** almost there buddy! Tell him to get his favorite. Spare no expense.

**@MatthewBarnett** have a 'gift' at register waiting. Mom is grabbing clothes! They don't know! You're gonna make us all cry

Mom just said she hasn't bought clothes in a long time she wants to cry. Wait until we get to register we'll all cry. Maybe I can live stream

As Barnett and Horvath helped the family, Horvath began taking video clips, and then live-streaming the action on UStream, ultimately putting the shots together to create a YouTube video. The encouraging Tweets he received were overwhelming.

Horvath's story shows how seeking help on Twitter is a great way to find much-needed resources. As we'll explore in the next chapter, the idea of reaching out to those who may be able to help you on Twitter is a great one. Twitter allows you access to people outside of your social graph, and non-profit organizations can take advantage of this to reach the influencers they need to engage.

Twitter also offers the unique ability to do personalized fundraising. The best fundraising comes through personal connections, and Twitter allows organizations to benefit from a broadened reach of personal asks.

Luke Renner and his family administer the day-to-day operations for The Caribbean Institute of Media Technologies, The Learning Village, and HANDS Across Haiti. When Renner came to visit Twitter headquarters in San Francisco in 2010, he told a powerful story of direct fundraising on Twitter. Because Renner is known in his Haitian community for his charitable efforts, one day a man knocked on his front door, asking for help to pay his daughter's school fees, which he himself couldn't afford. Renner turned to Twitter, and within hours was able to raise the necessary funds to send the young woman to school.

Connecting individuals with resources also works on Twitter on a mass scale, and broad humanitarian crises and emergency situations have shown how useful Twitter can be. The tragic earthquake in Haiti showed many examples of this.

## Using Twitter in Haiti

### by Luke Renner, Founder of Fireside International

On January 12, 2010, the day of Haiti's catastrophic earthquake, at 4:53 PM, when our house began to shudder around us along the northern coast of Haiti, Twitter entered back into our lives in a radical way. In that moment, when all of Haiti's phones were instantly taken offline and communication with others was brought to a standstill, it was my dormant Twitter account that connected our organization to the outside world and ushered in a fundamental change in the way that we operate.

In those first moments, the job was simply to find out what was going on, to place ourselves within the greater context of events, and get a grasp on what was at stake. Twitter proved to be the only way to do this quickly and comprehensively. Beyond just sending and receiving emails within our own circles, we were now using Twitter to communicate with a broad range of people we had never met (some who are now dear friends), each offering more clarity and form to what would otherwise have been sheer madness.

After finding our place within the evolving narrative, we began adding our own experiences from the ground. By morning, I had tweeted our VOIP number, talked with @anncurry on the phone, distributed some of the first video from Haiti, and given countless interviews to a number of major international news agencies, each from the links we had distributed via Twitter. For no other reason than our connection to Twitter, we were providing information to a world that was hungry to engage.

I have personally participated in and witnessed numerous exchanges on Twitter that have undoubtedly led to the extension of time, opportunity, quality of life, and (I believe) life itself for those on the receiving end in Haiti.

Twitter truly is a great leveler. Because of Twitter's ability to place everyone onto a common stage, direct and publicly accessible discourse is available to any and all who have interest in a cause and the time to devote.

**Does Twitter Save Lives?**
It's a popular question but a poorly crafted one. It's like asking a blacksmith if heat makes horseshoes. The answer is both "yes" and "no." The heat is certainly a critical component, but to give the heat full credit for the creation of the horseshoe is nonsense.

Before broaching this question, I reached out to several of my Twitter colleagues from the months immediately following the earthquake about their experiences. Overwhelmingly, the response was that the majority of the heavy lifting in any life-saving circumstance was done in person, over the phone, and/or through email. Their answers were in no way shocking; as it turns out, that was my experience too. In fact, in all of my time moving through the epicenter after the disaster, Twitter never once handed someone a bottle of water, a plate of food, or any life-saving medicine. Twitter was not standing there when baby Landina was reunited with her mother after a six-month separation. Twitter did not deliver tents or chop away at the piles of concrete.

What Twitter did do was rapidly connect people from drastically different walks of life—perfect strangers with incredibly diverse experience, capabilities, and resources. And it was precisely those connections that gave birth to the kinds of exchanges that inevitably and repeatedly materialized into life-saving results (like bottles of water, food, medical attention, and other practical advances). Twitter repeatedly served as the catalyst that launched potential energy into kinetic action and transformed the common person into a powerhouse of positive social change.

Growing up in the ghettos of Baltimore, Lynette Camara thought she understood the meaning of being poor until her uncle sent her pictures of an orphanage he was working at in Haiti. Since seeing those images, Camara has made it her mission to help others to break free of poverty. She is the creator and founder of USAforHaiti and an advisor to Kledev, an organization that empowers economic development in Haiti. Although she wasn't on the ground when the earthquake happened, she was able to use the tools at her disposal far away from the disaster area to help. Her efforts also show how connecting resources through data mining is a growing field in humanitarian aid work. When she learned from her uncle that the landlines were down but the Internet was working, she quickly got in touch with @carelpedre, a radio personality in Haiti who was able to get messages out using his equipment, and @ramhaiti (Richard Morse), a hotel owner and musician who also had access to computer equipment and was posting crucial information. Camara created a database that matched information about those who were alive with those looking for them. She explains,

> If the database got a match by name, age, location, or other identifying information, I would try to further verify that information. When I was sure there was a match, I would send out a Tweet to announce it. Then, once verified (for as much as it was possible to verify information coming out of Haiti in those days), I would post the information I received directly to Twitter, the feed of which was running on my website.
>
> It became apparent that not only were there people searching for information on missing loved ones or posting that they were alive and well in Haiti, but there were many postings from people still in need of rescuing. Many of them were text messages sent to Twitter so that they would show up online. I saw on CNN that the Germans had a satellite trained on Haiti in order to map the changes in topography due to the earthquake.

Camara got access to their satellite so she could communicate with the people online claiming to be trapped or hungry to map their GPS coordinates into the satellite and get a high resolution photo of the area to study in order to find out whether there was anything that might prevent access, such as roads blocked by debris or cracks in the ground. In turn, she relayed the information to authorities on the ground. Ultimately, she says, "I collected as much information as possible from all around the Internet, ran it through my database to try and match information from survivors with posts from people looking for survivors, and fed it through one website, www.usaforhaiti.org, via a Twitter feed."

Gretchen Steidle Wallace, the founder and CEO of Global Grassroots, is another individual who used the power of Twitter to make connections during the earthquake. While living and working at the site of a collapsed hotel, she helped family members overseas and rescue workers on the ground to connect during relief efforts through her handle, @consciouschange.

1:27 PM Jan 22nd, 2010 via UberTwitter

**@ConsciousChange**

Word is Hatiian govt may call off search & rescue today, but US continuing at Hotel Montana. We're here at that operation. #Haiti

http://twitter.com/ConsciousChange/status/8075165624

1:55 AM Jan 23rd, 2010 via UberTwitter

**@ConsciousChange**

Canadians needing info: 1-800-267-6788 or todd.stewart@international.gc.ca. All those names I shared have confirmed open cases with Embassy.

http://twitter.com/ConsciousChange/status/8100020330

In the aftermath of the 2011 earthquake and tsunami in Japan, similar relief efforts occurred.

## Using Twitter in Japan

By James Kondo, manager of Twitter in Japan and World
Economic Forum Young Global Leader

On March 11, 2011, the biggest earthquake in a thousand years struck Northeastern Japan. Tsunamis washed away entire communities. Nuclear power plants were destroyed. Over twenty-eight thousand people have died or are still missing.

In the hours, days, and weeks after the earthquake, Twitter's life-saving potential in global emergencies was borne out.

1. *Reaching loved ones:* Scenes right after the earthquake showed people frantically trying to call their family and friends on mobile phones — but in vain. The mobile network was down, and would take several hours to come back on. However, one thing was up and running throughout the crisis: Twitter. Twitter users could tweet, follow, and send direct messages. Those who realized that Twitter was active quickly signed up.
2. *Getting critical information:* In times of emergency, events unfold quickly. Consequences could be deadly or life-saving. Real-time Tweets provided by the government and news agencies, updated on a minute-by-minute basis, became critical sources of information.
3. *Mapping the situation and solutions:* Within minutes, a whole array of hashtags were deployed to help map the situation and find solutions. For example, #j_j_helpme Tweets enabled stranded citizens to be geolocated onto a map and rescued. #311care Tweets provided essential medical information for those injured and sick. Hashtags evolved to address the most pertinent issues, and provide real-time problem solving.

In our everyday life, Twitter is a simple, smart, intuitive tool to follow your interests. In times of emergency, there is another layer of Twitter that saves lives.

In a world with so many emergencies born of natural and unnatural disasters — earthquakes, hurricanes, tsunamis, terrorism, wars, famines, and droughts, just to mention some — there is a whole new role for Twitter to play.

"Twitter as a lifeline" — That's the role Twitter can play to help those who are suffering the most in times of their greatest need.

In the wake of the quake and tsunamis, without power and regular access to the Internet, Twitter via mobile was more active than ever. Jeannie Stamberger, associate director of Carnegie Mellon University's Disaster Management Initiative (DMI), was quoted saying that more than 1,200 Tweets per minute were coming from Tokyo within an hour after the magnitude 9.0 earthquake. Stamberger said, "The amount of data flowing over social media during this crisis has been overwhelming." (see http://www.cmu.edu/homepage/society/2011/winter/siliconvalley-dmi.shtml).

In one case, the NBC *Today Show*'s Ann Curry helped find one lost American in Japan. When Twitter user Megan Walsh asked Ann Curry (via Tweet) to find her sister, @anncurry tweeted back that she would try to help.

13 Mar via Twitter for BlackBerry®

**@AnnCurry**

@wednesdaywalsh the link won't open for me here. If you could dm me details, I will do my best.

http://twitter.com/#!/AnnCurry/status/47094981286047744

A day later, on Monday, March 14, Curry and her crew traveled to a middle school in the town of Minamisanriku, where the missing American Canon Purdy used to teach and where she was on the day of the earthquake. Finding her alive and well, they immediately put Purdy in touch with her family in the United States—who had been waiting for seventy-two hours for word from her.

## Tweets as Data: The Present and Future
## of Crisis Mapping

The use of Twitter via mobile and SMS in disaster relief is not just about sending and receiving information, but also about tracking and plotting those reports so that people have accurate information, and so that relief organizations can respond. Crisis maps are tools that plot reports coming from a variety of sources (SMS, RSS, Tweets, and the like)— and allow for action. Noel Dickover, cofounder of Crisis Commons, explains, "Twitter provides a valuable tool for crisis mappers early on in a disaster because it allows local participants to quickly communicate both the overall state of the disaster and details of a specific event (e.g., 'My son is trapped in this building . . . '). This dynamic allows the larger crowd to find and aggregate these Tweets through various crisis mapping platforms."

Ushahidi is one of the most prominent of the crisis mapping organizations at work today. In Kiswahili, *ushahidi* means "to bear witness," and the organization got its start when serving as an important way for individuals on the ground to document post-election violence during the highly disputed Kenyan presidential elections in late 2007. Thanks to Ushahidi's crisis mapping of the violent demonstrations in the slums, the outside world got a grasp of the severity of the situation. Patrick Meier, director of crisis mapping at Ushahidi and a Ph.D. fellow at Stanford University's Program on Liberation Technologies, says simply: "Crisis mapping is about creating live maps of the world around us." These maps democratize information, increase transparency, and lower the barriers for individuals to share their stories, ultimately allowing humanitarian aid organizations to provide relief based on the geo-coordinates of a report. In Meier's eyes, crisis maps like the one used in Japan (see Figure 4.1) "are to humanitarian crises what X-rays are to hospital ERs." As a result, many organizations throughout the world—Twitter included—are eager to work with crisis mappers like Ushahidi in disaster situations.

12:43 PM Jan 28th, 2010 via UberTwitter

**@ConsciousChange**

Hoping to work with Ushahidi to create advanced site to handle aid needs/distribution, volunteers and alarms. Stay tuned. #Haiti

http://twitter.com/ConsciousChange/status/8327054199

18 Mar via web

**@PatrickMeier**

Japan Crisis Map (http://www.sinsai.info/ushahidi) is being accessed from 70+ countries with 70%+ hits coming from #Japan #jpeq

http://twitter.com/#!/PatrickMeier/status/48784008166916096

The strategy of formally collecting information gained from many sources (including Tweets) and then connecting those in need of resources with those who can help is one that we've worked on at Twitter headquarters. In October of 2010, nine months after Haiti's devastating earthquake, Haiti was plagued by another crisis: a cholera outbreak.

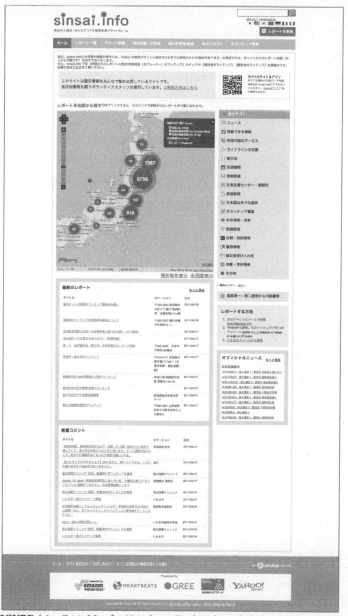

**FIGURE 4.1** Crisis Map for 2011 Japan Earthquake and Nuclear Crisis. SOURCE: http://tmappsevents.esri.com/EQJapan/index.html. Map data © OpenStreetMap contributors, CC-BY-SA.

International aid organizations worked hard to provide support to victims as the disease spread from the outskirts into the capital city. Building off of Twitter's use in the Haiti earthquake, the American Red Cross worked with us at Twitter to onboard a new account, @kwawouj, that sent updates in Haitian Creole directing individuals to the resources they needed. Working with mobile carriers in Haiti, Voila, one of Haiti's largest mobile providers, generously pushed out an SMS message in Haitian Creole to all Voila's mobile users, encouraging them to follow @kwawouj's cholera update Tweets via SMS. Crisis mappers then stepped in. With the cholera outbreak, HealthMap, an openly available public health intelligence system similar to Ushahidi, provided the element shown in Figure 4.2.

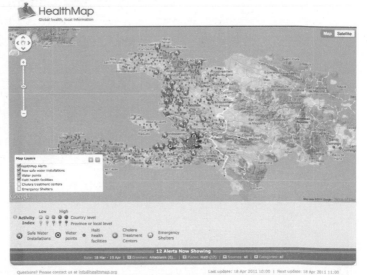

**FIGURE 4.2** Health Map's Crisis Map for Haiti Cholera Outbreak. SOURCE: http://healthmap.org/hope140/index.php

The limits of such resource mapping do not stop with crisis management, however, and Ushahidi and other crisis mapping organizations have been used in increasing ways to create awareness through data mining and data plotting. Following up on the 2009 success of turning the Twitter platform red on World AIDS Day, in 2010 the product partnering program (RED) envisioned another way to make a large-scale impact. For World AIDS Day in 2010, (RED) engaged Ushahidi to develop a unique world map. As Chrysi Philalithes, director of digital and strategy marketing at (RED) explains, the map proved the epitome of engagement. Each time someone tweeted using #turnred on World AIDS Day, the message mapped itself onto a data visualizer of the world. Each action served to turn a different time zone on the map red (see Figure 4.3).

In the wake of the massive earthquake and tsunamis in Japan, other new initiatives sprang up. Carnegie Mellon University's Ian Lane, an assistant research professor in Silicon Valley, helped to map critical Tweets. Lane told

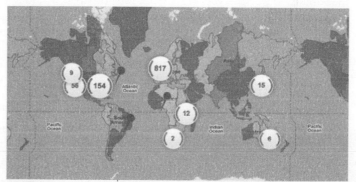

**FIGURE 4.3** #turnred Ushahidi and (RED) worked together on World AIDS Day 2010.

CMU.edu, "With the help of volunteers, within a few hours we had developed an architecture for the live monitoring of Twitter as well as a basic system to automatically identify the most critical Tweets from the huge volume that were being generated." The CMU group then built a "Twitter parsing" system in Japanese to extract the location and person's name from each Tweet. After verifying the data, they entered it into Google Person Finder, allowing people all over the world to check in and see whether friends and family in Japan were safe. Lane said that the model "bridges the gap between unstructured social media and structured data." He continued, "Just by tweeting a message stating that they are fine and well, this information will become available to all their friends and family around the world via Google Person Finder." (See http://www.cmu.edu/homepage/society/ 2011/winter/siliconvalley-dmi.shtml.)

Efforts like these are examples of the innovative ways that people use Twitter to engage in situations where information is more important than ever. Although crisis-mapping tools that collate data received via SMS and plot it on interactive maps provide an important step in connecting resources with those who need them, they also bring up concerns. When Jon Gosier, director of product for the SwiftRiver open source platform at Ushahidi, came into Twitter headquarters, I asked him what he thought of the criticism that it is difficult to prove the veracity of the reports when using crisis mapping. Jon candidly explained,

> There's two ways I think about this question. First is from
> a technical level, the integrity of the information itself, and
> proving validity. That's exceedingly difficult for machines

to do because it requires an understanding of things beyond the information itself. Context about an event, language, intent, motive . . . all these things play into verifying information. If someone sends a message that says, "My house is on fire," without additional context there is no way to verify [that] what was said is either true or false.

The other way I think about this is from the crowd-sourcing perspective. Platforms like Ushahidi and Twitter lower the bar for everyone to communicate freely. It's in the participation of the many that they are most effective. So in some ways having unvalidated information is the point. Making communication accessible to all is first, keeping participation high is second . . . if you have those first two, I think the process of prioritizing who to listen to (validated versus unvalidated members of the crowd) becomes a good problem to have. Because you'll only be concerned about malicious content if there's an overabundance of participation to begin with.

It's true. If the goal is open information, then "unvalidated" information just may be the whole point. Ideally, the future will see further integration of Twitter emergency messages, mobile carrier announcements, and crisis mapping.

## Top Questions About the "Engage" Step

Q: What if someone says something negative about my organization?

A: The beauty of Twitter is in the increased transparency of information. There are downsides, however, and some individuals have a hard time adjusting to an era in which employees have the freedom to tweet, rather than the traditional filtering of any and all statements made by an organization through a communications or public relations team.

One of the great capabilities of Twitter is the chance to see what others are saying about you and to jump in on the conversation and correct them if you feel the wrong impression about you is being perpetrated. Customer service and donor relations have never been more high touch, and the best thing your organization can do is to take advantage of these abilities to make transparency your friend. If someone says something negative about you, enter the conversation and work to correct their opinion. John Carnell, founder and CEO of Stop Bullying, argues, "You can't please everyone, so don't worry when you don't—Twitter is all about people's viewpoints. You're not always going to agree, and I can guarantee you will meet followers who hold the absolute polar view to your [organization's mission] or subject matter. You *must* stay focused on your brand's core values when this happens and be ready to agree to disagree. Tweet Wars help no one, least of all your brand." He does add, however, "When you get it wrong, apologize! Everyone makes mistakes but having the bottle to admit those mistakes publicly can be difficult for the soul. We are all human, and it's easy to say the wrong thing in the heat of the Tweet."

Q: Who should monitor my organization's Twitter
account?

A: Although I know many organizations with multiple
individuals handling their Twitter accounts, and
this can be necessary at times, I do believe that the
individual doing most of the tweeting should be
the one involved in responding to account issues and
monitoring the account. Remember, the goal with
any organizational account is to keep it personal
and up-to-date enough to maintain the interest and
involvement of donors and supporters. This will
(usually) be more likely to happen if one person
owns the project.

Q: Are Twitter parties a good way to promote engagement?

A: Twitter parties are becoming more and more popular as a way to bring Twitter followers together and
to promote an upcoming event or campaign. Typically, a Twitter party involves at least one organization (although it can include many) coming together
to tweet about a particular issue for a set amount of
time—say, one hour on Thursday night. Twitter
parties use one hashtag and encourage participation from the audience in the form of questions,
auction bidding, and raffle drawings. Non-profits
considering a Twitter party should be very clear with
themselves whether or not their true goal is fundraising, as that adds in more complicated elements that

must be accounted for. In brief, when doing a live auction or raffle over Twitter, it is essential that you can trust the followers who are participating.

Although it may seem like a strange tactic, you should also consider having a private Twitter party—a Twitter party on a protected account. Although this limits the attendees and restricts the buzz you can generate on Twitter, it would allow for certain financial issues to be easier. Twitter parties should always have an agenda and a clear timekeeper. It's easy for things to get out of hand, and it's best to ensure you have a plan for what actions your followers should take at various points throughout the party.

**WEB**

See more information about Twitter parties at http://twitter4good.com/resources/twitter-parties/

Q:  What about Tweet-ups?

A:  Tweet-ups are similar to Twitter parties, but they happen in person, and non-profit organizations sometimes find these more useful for promoting donor engagement. With a Tweet-up, you can not only encourage your supporters to tweet about your cause but also introduce elements that exist in a regular fundraising party. There is growing interest in this form, as it brings together virtual and in-person efforts. As with Twitter parties, make sure that your organization has an active, engaged account and that you continue to keep it active following the event.

Q: All these suggestions are well and good, but what I really need is *one million followers*. Once I have *one million followers*, then I'll start implementing your ideas. *Can you help me get one million followers?*

A: Whenever someone asks me this question, I cringe. It's a huge mistake to think you need tons of followers to reach your goals on Twitter.

Scott Stratten, president of UnMarketing, tells a fantastic story about what true engagement is. After making a parody video called "Why Don't You Leave Me Alone: A Facebook Song," he tweeted out the link from his account @unmarketing (see http://bit.ly/OutOfTune). With forty-five thousand followers at the time, he tracked that twelve thousand clicked on the link. The next day, Ashton Kutcher tweeted the same link. It also got clicked about twelve thousand times. How many followers did Ashton have? Four and a half million. As Stratten says, "It shows that engagement of your audience is more important than sheer numbers."

Furthermore, influential Tweets can come from anyone. One of the most famous Tweets of 2011 came from @keithurbahn, chief of staff to former U.S. secretary of defense Donald Rumsfeld.

**@Keithurbahn**

So I'm told by a reputable person they have killed Osama Bin Laden. Hot damn.

http://twitter.com/#!/keithurbahn/status/64877790624886784

SocialFlow, a social media optimization platform, did an extensive analysis of the Tweet to better understand its staggering spread over the Web. As they estimate, "Within a minute, more than 80 people had already reposted the message, including the NYTimes reporter Brian Stelter. Within two minutes, over 300 reactions to the original post were spreading . . . The actual number of impressions (people who saw Keith's message in their stream but didn't repost it) is substantially higher" (see http://blog.socialflow.com/post/5246404319/breaking-bin-laden-visualizing-the-power-of-a-single). There's no telling how many millions ultimately saw his message.

Do you know how many followers Urbahn had when he tweeted it?

1,106.

# E (Explore): Finding Everybody, and Bringing Everybody to You

# 5

No one wants to tweet in a bubble. One way to ensure that your Tweets are not only reaching more individuals, but are also encompassing increasingly relevant topics, is to consistently look for new information, new followers, and new influencers on Twitter. Let's explore some of the best ways to do so.

## Finding Yourself

Once your organization is on Twitter, it's essential to regularly search for mentions of the organization. By finding out what others are saying about you, you can connect with individuals who already like you. You can even try to change the minds of those who don't. In sum, searching for yourself will help you do three important things:

1. Strengthen relationships with existing supporters
2. Convert a potential supporter to an existing supporter
3. Provide reputation management or convert a negative opinion

While living in Kenya during my early months on Twitter, I tweeted about the daily happenings of my non-profit organization. At the time, however, I was using an account not named for Hope Runs. Looking back, I'm sure it was confusing for followers. By the time I decided to eventually streamline things, simple searching showed me that there was indeed another non-profit organization in the world named Hope Runs that was using the @hoperuns handle. I regretted my early branding mistakes, and I lamented the number of potential supporters I had likely lost by not searching and remedying the problem sooner. So I made a change. Despite the exposure my account had gotten in the early days—making the Twitter blog, and landing a shout-out on the homepage of the early Twitter—I eventually changed gears, changed Twitter handles, and pushed forward a newly branded account.

In addition to doing such a simple search for an overlapping name, you want to ensure that you are searching Twitter regularly to hear the latest things people are saying about your organization. In searching for her organization, Danielle Brigida of the National Wildlife Federation was able to help turn a frustrated supporter into a happy one. One day, she came upon a potential supporter complaining about the National Wildlife Federation, specifically saying

that she was not able to buy a magazine subscription online
due to website problems:

about 1 hour ago via HootSuite

Dear National Wildlife Federation, I would happily
renew my kids magazine subscriptions if your site
worked.

Brigida responded right away, fixing the follower's problem and immediately earning this Tweet from the now happy
user:

14 minutes ago via HootSuite

National Wildlife Federation magazine resubscribe
success! :) Great magazines for kids. http://
ow.ly/1tema

There's no better way to earn a great opinion of your
organization than to listen when others are talking about
you and jump in with a response to solve their problems.

Doing daily searches or setting up an automatic search
feed is also an excellent practice for the individual in your organization who takes on the more formalized role of customer
support. Melanie Mathos of Blackbaud offers a non-profit
spin on a successful customer service story using Twitter.

When a customer popped up in the Blackbaud search
feed one day, frustrated with one of their products, Mathos
proactively reached out to him and provided support. His
response? A big thanks—more than once—sent via Twitter, saying that @melmatho was indeed "faster than our
account rep!" The lesson was valuable for Blackbaud. Mathos

says, "We value being not only responsive as a support organization but also proactive when it comes to addressing
customers' issues. We are now taking that a step further and
are creating a dedicated support account on Twitter to
further enhance the support experience."

Leila Janah of Samasource says that searching on Twitter
helps her organization "keep track of trends in our market
space, like the latest in social enterprise, the growth in social
capital markets, and news about areas we work in, like Africa.
We can search from the Twitter home page for new topics
or trends we hear about, or we can bookmark a search in our
favorite desktop app. We can also share search terms and
hashtags with our community."

In short, you don't know where you stand on Twitter if
you don't look (out) for yourself.

## Finding Key Endorsements and New Leads

As you Explore, you should also be looking for new
endorsements and leads that might propel your organization
to the next level. Twitter allows you to be in contact with
anyone—no matter who they are—and the possibilities
this presents are limitless. The previous chapter discussed
the idea that non-profit organizations should make private
lists of journalists, public relations representatives, and
other influencers to follow. Over time, organizations can
then begin conversations with these individuals to build
relationships that will ultimately help their causes.

Global Citizen Year, the non-profit organization that
sends high school graduates on year-long apprenticeships in

developing countries, is full of active Twitter participants. Their CEO, Abby Falik, became a Twitter fan when she realized its power for connecting causes with influencers. Falik says she was not thoroughly convinced of the power of Twitter for organizations until Twitter sparked an ongoing relationship—and a key endorsement—from *New York Times* journalist Nick Kristof.

Falik had always known that the two-time Pulitzer Prize–winning journalist was interested in issues of global education:

> I've always been a huge admirer of Nick Kristof, and the ways he uses his skill and influence to shine a massive spotlight on critical global issues that would otherwise go unseen. Kristof has often written about the need to get more Americans overseas, arguing that if more people in this country had the opportunity to see global poverty firsthand, there would be a shift from an era of American apathy toward one defined by responsible global engagement. At the same time, he has been a vocal advocate for the gap year as a unique opportunity for young people to see the world beyond our borders. Knowing his personal interests were so closely aligned with our mission at Global Citizen Year, I reached out—initially via Twitter!—to enlist him as an ally.

Let's look at the specifics of how Global Citizen Year found a true ally in a Twitter influencer. In the first stages of Global Citizen Year's time on Twitter, @globalcitizenyr began citing quotes and articles Kristof had written in the *New York Times* in Tweets. At this early point, Global Citizen Year was still new on Twitter and was not yet using Nick Kristof's Twitter handle when they referred to him:

20 May 09 via Ping.fm

**@GlobalCitizenYr**

"some time at the grassroots is an invaluable addition to classroom learning" - Kristof - http://ping.fm/ZlqpY

http://twitter.com/#!/GlobalCitizenYr/status/1864880251

Once Falik found him on Twitter and started following him, @globalcitizenyr began to send him Tweets via @reply to his then-handle, @nytimeskristof:

18 Sep 09 via Ping.fm

**@GlobalCitizenYr**

@nytimeskristof & let's make it before college when young people are still forming their senses of themselves in the world -Global Citi ...

http://twitter.com/#!/GlobalCitizenYr/status/4082946438

Over time, @globalcitizenyr began retweeting Kristof's Tweets in which he mentioned issues they had in common. Kristof's own son was pursuing a "gap year" before college, and Kristof regularly wrote about other young adults spending time in the developing world, including the Congo:

29 Oct 09 via TweetDeck

**@GlobalCitizenYr**

RT @nytimeskristof: More young Americans should spend time in the dev world. Here's the blog of H. McConnell, in Congo: http://bit.ly/3nbNJM

http://twitter.com/#!/GlobalCitizenYr/status/5268416432

Seeing his support of that student in the Congo, and reading his passion for gap years in general in his best-selling book *Half the Sky*, Global Citizen Year crafted a blog post addressing these connections and tweeted it out (see http://globalcitizenyear.org/2010/01/kristof-voices-support-for-bridge-year-in-half-the-sky/).

11 Jan 9 via TweetDeck

**@GlobalCitizenYr**

Kristof voices support for bridge year in "Half the Sky." Read a few excerpts on our blog - http://bit.ly/4Kaola

http://twitter.com/#!/GlobalCitizenYr/status/7642792877

At some point Kristof took notice and began retweeting GCYTweets via his new account @nickkristof. Over time, he even began writing Tweets of his own that promoted Global Citizen Year, praising Global Citizen Year and linking to the GCY homepage:

16 Dec 09 via TweetDeck

**@GlobalCitizenYr**

RT @NickKristof: Impressive effort to give young people a gap year to learn about the world, get skills to save it: http://bit.ly/7JIdZZ

http://twitter.com/#!/GlobalCitizenYr/status/6736042083

Wil Keenan, then communications and technology manager at Global Citizen Year, said that a thousand people clicked through the Tweet to see what Global Citizen Year was all about. A few months later, Kristof went on to feature Global Citizen Year in a *New York Times* article he wrote about the importance of Americans spending time in other cultures. GCY then tweeted:

11 Mar via TweetDeck

**@GlobalCitizenYr**

Kristof cites GCY as he stresses the need 4 Americans 2 embed in other cultures - it's a national priority http://nyti.ms/aUhmOT

http://twitter.com/#!/GlobalCitizenYr/status/10332879620

Following the publication of the article, Global Citizen Year went a step further: a GCY fellow in the field wrote her own response to Kristof's *New York Times* piece. @globalcitizenyr tweeted it, making sure to include Kristof's Twitter handle in the Tweet to get his notice:

23 Mar via TweetDeck

**@GlobalCitizenYr**

Fellow, Gaya Morris responds to @NickKristof in her post discussing education & the teacher shortage in Senegal http://bit.ly/90Dxi1

http://twitter.com/#!/GlobalCitizenYr/status/10942387178

And notice it he did. He immediately wrote his own Tweet promoting fellow Gaya Morris's blog post.

24 Mar via web

**@NickKristof**

An American student teaching in Senegal responds to my "Teach for the World" proposal http://bit.ly/90Dxi1

http://twitter.com/#!/NickKristof/status/10973051527

Global Citizen Year was careful to highlight each effort Kristof made to promote them on their own end as well—always making sure to retweet the Tweets he sent out about them for the benefit of their followers:

24 Mar via TweetDeck

**@GlobalCitizenYr**

RT @NickKristof: An American student teaching in Senegal responds to my "Teach for the World" proposal http://bit.ly/90Dxi1

http://twitter.com/#!/GlobalCitizenYr/status/10982610964

The relationship continued, and Global Citizen Year kept reaching out:

30 July via TweetDeck

**@GlobalCitizenYr**

@nickkristof: Every child on earth could get a primary ed for the cost of 5 wks military spend in Afghanistan: http://nyti.ms/brIIoV

http://twitter.com/#!/GlobalCitizenYr/status/19914803675

Kristof continued to highlight them:

19 Oct via bitly

**@NickKristof**

Sage advice from a young American on her gap year in Senegal: http://bit.ly/9X4HMy

http://twitter.com/#!/NickKristof/status/27858608812

And they continued to thank him for his promotion:

19 Oct via TweetDeck

**@GlobalCitizenYr**

A must-read post by Fellow, Tess Langan RT
@NickKristof: Sage advice from a young American
on her gap year in Senegal: http://bit.ly/9X4HMy

http://twitter.com/#!/GlobalCitizenYr/status/27861834112

Nearly a year after the relationship had first come to
fruition on Twitter, Global Citizen Year fellow Tess Langan
wrote her own *New York Times* piece about why she had put
off attending Colgate College to spend a year in Senegal:

5 Nov via TweetDeck

**@GlobalCitizenYr**

Fellow, Tess Langan in her piece in the @nytimes "I
am spending my year in Senegal. College will have
to wait." http://nyti.ms/9p1dH7

http://twitter.com/#!/GlobalCitizenYr/status/692867492225024

Kristof continued to cheer them on:

14 Dec via TweetDeck

**@GlobalCitizenYr**

In his Sunday column, @NickKristof recommends
Global Citizen Year for students looking to take a
gap year - http://nyti.ms/grSGek

http://twitter.com/#!/GlobalCitizenYr/status/14799381857304576

When I asked Kristof about Global Citizen Year reaching
out via Twitter, he said, "I always hear from young people
who want to go abroad but think it's unaffordable or too
dangerous, or their parents are aghast at the idea. So when I

heard of an organization working to address those concerns, backed by someone with Abby's credentials, I wanted to help spread the word." He added that this wasn't the first time this has happened to him: "Something similar happened with Givology (@givology), by the way. I think I found out about them elsewhere, but then I became aware of their Twitter presence and followed them. That led to occasionally retweeting them or highlighting their work. And following them certainly put them more on my front burner than they ever would be otherwise."

Ultimately, this step-by-step example of how Global Citizen Year developed, expanded, and maximized a relationship with a key influencer like Nick Kristof shows just how to best use Twitter to Explore potential powerful connections.

### How to Contact Influencers on Twitter

Tim Ferriss (@tferriss), angel investor (Twitter, StumbleUpon, Evernote, and others) and author of the number one *New York Times* bestsellers *The 4-Hour Body* and *The 4-Hour Workweek*, gets tons of @replies, retweets, and DMs on Twitter that encourage him to support worthy causes. He has a few tips on filtering out the good from the rest:

> *Make it specific and offer proof you're capable or credible.*
>
> "@tferriss You can help Darfur—please retweet this link to raise funds!" will not get looked at, as it sounds like every other pitch and requires me to do too much homework.

More effective, here's a total hypothetical: "@tferriss I work with the United Nations; here's how I used your 4HWW principles in Africa: bit.ly/africatf"

*Keep it to 120 or less, and get your friends to retweet it.*

For your message to stand out in the firehose stream of Tweets, I first need to see it. If your Tweet is 137 characters, no one can easily retweet without editing. The hypothetical I just offered is less than 120 characters.

*Use multiple channels.*

The easiest way to influence me is to have one of my friends (*not* someone who's just met me once) email me and ask me to take a look at your work. For instance, the founders of The Do Lectures speaking series emailed me a link to a video of Maggie Doyne, a twenty-three-year-old American who set up a school in Nepal for two hundred orphans. She later tweeted at me, and I then retweeted a link to her video. Without the tee up, this wouldn't have happened. Maggie is very good with PR and soon thereafter appeared as the cover story of the *New York Times Magazine*.

## Finding New Supporters

Some of the influencers that organizations search for on Twitter will not be influential for the megaphone they provide, but rather for the direct resources they offer. There are many ways to find individual donors among those already interested in your cause on Twitter, and there is another untapped donor resource as well. Most large brands and small companies are on Twitter and have dedicated individuals working on this part of their new media strategy. Non-profit organizations can take advantage of this fact to find in-kind or monetary donors from big businesses in much the same way they can with private individuals. As the case of @aircanada and the broken wheelchair shows, brands are listening.

Luke Renner of Fireside International, a non-profit media company, has another powerful story of fundraising on Twitter—but the donation his organization received was not in the form of dollars. At Fireside International in Haiti, Luke Renner uses technology to improve the lives of the poor. In 2010, his technology school, The Caribbean Institute of Media Technologies, realized the importance of offering an English language class to their students. Deciding that Rosetta Stone offered the material his students would most benefit from, he looked into purchasing enough licenses for the product to teach it to the hundreds of students at his school. When he realized that it would cost $18,000 to buy enough Rosetta Stone materials to service all his students, he was heartbroken. He certainly didn't have that kind of money.

After determining that Rosetta Stone was on Twitter, he decided to craft a Tweet about his need for the materials. When @rosettastone responded, Renner soon landed a generous in-kind donation of all the materials he needed.

He was floored—and could be seen thanking @rosettastone throughout the year:

15 Nov via Twitter for iPad

**@firesideint**

Just cracked the box on some new language software. I'm telling you what, @RosettaStone cares about people! Thx for supporting us!

http://twitter.com/#!/firesideint/statuses/4326245072375808

25 Nov via TweetDeck

**@firesideint**

Happy #Thanksgiving to the folks @RosettaStone! We have MUCH to be grateful for because of you!

http://twitter.com/#!/firesideint/statuses/7733848217485312

Twitter is particularly effective when tapping into the local power of individual communities. Even if the cause is far away, a local event or campaign can generate interest. Fostering Opportunities for Refugee Growth and Empowerment (FORGE) is a small non-profit organization bent on transparency. Starting their Twitter account was a natural progression from the already frequent blogging that founder and CEO Kjerstin Erickson was already involved in at SocialEdge.org. When they were in the running for a small grant from the Jenzabar Foundation, Erickson knew just what to do. To get the requisite five hundred comments on her blog post entry, she tweeted about the experience. When they won, she let her followers know!

15 May 09 via web

**@Kjer**

Great news! Thanks for all your comments and support, FORGE was just announced as winner of the $3k Jenzabar Social Media Leadership Award!!!

http://twitter.com/#!/Kjor/ctatuc/1800757337

And when Erickson got buzz surrounding a series of blog posts she wrote about the financial troubles of FORGE in early 2009, Twitter helped. Any time she wrote a new post, her followers could be alerted right away to see the goods. For FORGE, Twitter also brings a local angle to international operations by making the issues as locally relevant as possible. With offices in Oakland, California and projects in Zambia, it takes a lot for FORGE to connect donors with their projects in the field. One approach is to bring locals together for fundraising events in their area. When World Refugee Day came around, FORGE tweeted out that they were looking for Bay Area artists and musicians for a local benefit they were holding.

21 Apr 09 via TweetDeck

**@Kjer**

RT @FORGE_vaughn:  Looking 4 Bay Area artists & musicians to take part in a 6.20.09 World Refugee Day benefit extravaganza. Send suggestions!

http://twitter.com/#!/Kjer/status/1578889575

Similarly, they send out Tweets asking locals to come out for neighborhood mixers.

12 May 09 via TweetDeck

**@Kjer**

RT @FORGE_vaughn:  SF friends- plz come hear about FORGE tonight @ Int'l Devlpmnt Network meetup. Mixer @6, prez @7. At Medjool in the mission!

http://twitter.com/#!/Kjer/status/1778002521

The goal is connecting, and many find that Twitter helps them do just that, no matter what country the user is in.

## The Power of Search and Promoted Tweets for Good

Another aspect of creating relevant Tweets is to understand what information others are searching for on Twitter (and on the Web—remember, your Tweets are searchable) and to show up in those searches.

In April 2010, Twitter launched its first advertising product with six businesses and two non-profit organizations: Partners in Health and Room to Read. The first product was called Promoted Tweets, a way to turn Tweets into paid advertisements based on targeted keywords Twitter users were searching for; Promoted Tweets for Good was the pro bono version. Our launch happened to coincide with the 2010 Skoll World Forum—where the nonprofit founders Paul Farmer and John Wood were in attendance. It was a busy week, and excellent timing for a new move within Twitter's nascent advertising product.

Our beta-testing non-profits, Room to Read and Partners in Health, were pioneers in jumping on board the new platform and testing its usage. As I formalized the Promoted

Tweets for Good pro bono program in the months that followed, we began systematically offering pro bono Promoted Tweets for Good to various non-profit organizations. We sought 501(c)(3) charitable organizations with a strong history of Twitter usage who had the bandwidth to take on the promoted Tweets campaign. We worked hard to time and place campaigns around important world events related to their cause. @join1goal ran during the World Cup, @kwawouj ran Red Cross emergency messages in Haitian Creole during the Cholera outbreak in Haiti, and @greaterthanaids ran their campaign on World Aids Day.

The morning of the earthquake and tsunami in Japan, I sought an English-language Twitter account that was serving consistent, relevant data that we could spotlight. @hawaiiredcross came recommended from multiple sources, and I quickly saw that their Twitter stream was full of useful advice and links to important resources. Even after being up all night, Cindy Tanaka from the Hawaii chapter of the American Red Cross worked with me to create the initial crisis Tweets campaign. Using keywords like earthquake, tsunami, japan, #tsunami, and #textredcross, the @hawaiiredcross-promoted Tweets sought to deliver relevant English-language information for those who were searching for it (via keyword) on Twitter.

39 minutes ago

🐦 **@HawaiiRedCross**

Looking 4 info on tsumani? @hawaiiredcross will be sharing info from other resources #tsunami #TextREDCROSS

Indeed, bidding on keywords—although always important in any such keyword-based ad platform—is even more critical when you need to coincide with exactly what people are searching for on Twitter. Understandably, campaigns that ran with highly searched items (such as @join1goal during the World Cup or @hawaiiredcross after the earthquake and tsunami in Japan) were able to garner high volumes of individuals exposed to their pro bono Promoted Tweets for Good.

Here's another example: Blog Action Day is a popular annual event each year in which bloggers around the world come together to blog about one cause for one day. In 2010, the issue was clean water, and Mike McCamon of Water.org saw that the Water.org account, @water, garnered 18.9M impressions in that five-day period on Twitter. "In fact, 17 percent of the traffic that included the #bad10 hashtag @water had either authored it or mentioned it. And fourteen of the top twenty-five retweeted Tweets were from @water," he said. All this taught him once again that people retweet interesting facts, "not self-promoting fluff."

Aside from such massive events, it is important to use valuable search terms on Twitter. Water.org was a recipient of Promoted Tweets for Good pro bono advertising (not during Blog Action Day), and McCamon explained that to find the best search terms for his campaigns, he used search.twitter.com and collected recent Tweets that mentioned @water, other water charities, and a few hash tags that @water occasionally used. He then followed the hashtags and inventoried all the Tweets from the campaign, remembering to look at user data to best see the reach of the campaign. "I've also done quite a bit of digging back down Twitter followings," he explained. "When I stopped, I had amassed about 1.5M users' info (number of followers, number of Tweets, etc.) from the collective following of @water and few others that have big followings in the NGO space." Ultimately, he learned what resonated with people and used that to help his Promoted Tweets for Good campaigns succeed—even without the boost of a popular event.

Although promoted products like Promoted Tweets will change over time, the value in understanding what individuals are looking for on Twitter will remain an important issue.

## New Examples of Success

A final step in the Explore aspect of the T.W.E.E.T. model is ensuring that your organization is keeping up to date on the latest trends and changes in advocacy and activism on Twitter. There are a host of excellent blogs on this topic, and www.Hope140.org is the official site that Twitter provides to help organizations and causes to better understand how to use Twitter. You'll find case studies, how-to materials, and cause campaigns we've worked on to get ideas.

See a list of some of the best blogs focused on Twitter at  http://twitter4good.com/resources/best-twitter-blogs/   **WEB**

Finding a Twitter mentor is also a great idea. I often recommend that non-profit accounts who want to learn to excel on Twitter look for popular accounts in their space to follow and then work to emulate their actions. This is a fast way to learn the ins and outs of how to best position yourself on Twitter. Modeling your behavior after those who are using it successfully is an easy way to get going quickly in the right direction.

## Top Questions on the "Explore" Step

Q:  How do I find the influencers?

A:  There are a few great ways to find influencers on Twitter. First, be sure to check out Twitter's Suggested User Lists in various categories. Individuals with high follower numbers and high engagement make it onto this list via an algorithm so these are all great examples of popular users in a given area of influence. Searching for highly followed lists is another fantastic way to find the movers and shakers in your area of interest, and you can set up automatic searches for keywords and phrases to help you find out who is interacting about given terms.

I've also suggested making your own private lists of influencers you are following. Consider choosing one or two of these influencers a week to focus on, and read all their @replies on any given day. There are many tools that can help you set up an automatic stream of who they are @replying to. This allows you to see who they are interacting with and will lead you to new influencers.

Q: Once I find the influencers, what's the best way to contact them via Twitter?

  A: It can be intimidating to contact influencers, and
     knowing how to do it well is the key to getting
     noticed by the people you are trying to woo. Check
     out the specific tips from Tim Ferriss earlier in
     the chapter.

# 6

# T (Track):
# Making Sure You've
# Hit Your Mark

I n this final step of the T.W.E.E.T. model, we'll look at the importance of *Tracking* to measure your target and to see the progress you are making or the areas in which you need to improve.

## Do You Remember Your Target?

As we explored in Chapter Two, there are three main types of *Targets* that non-profits typically set for themselves on Twitter: an *information account* like @roomtoread (which is an information hub for global literacy), a *personalized account* like @johnwoodr2r (the Room to Read CEO's personal take on his life as the CEO of a large non-profit), and a *fundraising account*, like @twestival.

In the T.W.E.E.T. model, there are two steps to tracking your progress toward these Targets.

## Step 1

After you identified your Target in Chapter Two, I asked you to choose five things you aimed to accomplish with your Target within six months.

It's time to look back at that list and see how you're doing. Did you meet any of these goals yet? Did any of these goals become irrelevant in the interim? Do the goals you set six months ago have a bearing on your current work? Looking at these earlier goals is a subjective, qualitative, but eye-opening experience. I hope that six months has been enough time for you to truly test out your strategy, but if you think you haven't given yourself enough time yet, simply wait a bit longer to track your progress again. After all, we're looking for improvement toward excellence, not self-flagellation.

## Step 2

After analyzing these specific goals you set for your account, we can now move onto more general metrics. The three main steps in the T.W.E.E.T. model—Write, Engage, Explore— serve as metric points in the tracking process. We can use each of these points to better judge exactly how effective a given account is. Here are some ideas of how to turn these guiding lights into specific, measurable points you can track to judge progress. To avoid overwhelm, choose a few metrics within each category that best apply to your organization that you'd like to track, and work on monitoring your progress in those metrics over time. Additionally, recognize that not all of these will be particularly relevant for every organizational account on Twitter, so ignore ones you think may not apply to you.

## Potential Metric Points to Measure:

*Write:*
- Number of Tweets per day/week/month
- Number of retweets sent
- Most retweeted Tweet
- Response to different types of Tweets
- Best Tweet
- Percentage of retweets sent to original Tweets
- Percentage of Tweets with media links
- Percentage of Tweets with photos
- Percentage of Tweets linking to organization website
- Percentage of Tweets linking to outside articles
- Existing memes
- Failed memes

*Engage:*
- Number of followers
- Number of following
- Number of retweets about your organization (analyze what was retweeted, when, and why)
- Number of @replies
- Number of @mentions
- Number of DMs

- Reach of a Tweet
- Follower growth rate
- Follower drop-off rate
- Most engaged day of the week
- Most engaged time of the day
- Number of lists on which your organization is placed as a list member

*Explore:*

- Number of lists following (lists your organization is following)
- Number of lists created (lists your organization created)
- Size and growth of lists created
- Mentions per day
- Retweets by influencers
- Reaction to retweets by influencers
- Press mentions of Twitter account (your Twitter handle should be included in articles about your organization, for example)
- Percentage of followers made up of "influencers"
- Number of influencers actively followed on your private "public relations" list
- New relationships created

Let's use these metric suggestions to examine what it means to track the three main Targets that organizational accounts typically set on Twitter: information accounts, personalized accounts, and fundraising accounts.

## Tracking an Information Account

After reviewing the questions you set for yourself to see where you stand six months after implementing your Target, it's time to move on to the standard metrics in the T.W.E.E.T. model—Write, Engage, Explore. Here are some of the common issues that come up in these metric points for information accounts.

- *Write: Quality, Activity*—An information account needs to remember to avoid creating too many updates, as that can lead to unfollows. It is also a good idea for information accounts to test slight increases in their information updates. For example, if @roomtoread currently sends ten Tweets per week, a good metric to explore would be whether or not their followers respond positively or negatively when they increase the number of Tweets sent by 30 to 50 percent. Many information accounts will also want to review their content to make sure they are keeping on track. Like @roomtoread, which sought to be a comprehensive information account about global literacy, many information accounts may be accompanied by secondary organizational accounts that have a different focus, like @johnwoodrtr, who aims to keep his Room to Read account more personal. Because information accounts are sometimes difficult to keep up due to the quantity of relevant information needed, it is easy for some information accounts to morph into personalized accounts. Make sure that if, say, your followers began following you because they want information on refugee transition programs in San Francisco, they don't end up finding that all your organizational Tweets are about your CEO's travels.

- *Engage: Activity, Modes of Interaction*—Engagement is simple to track numerically, and it is tempting for information accounts to track retweets of their informative messages. But a word of caution: information accounts should remember that it is not merely the volume of retweets, but the distance they travel that will make the difference in the long run.

- *Explore: Followers, Position, Growth*—Although an account with any of the three main account targets (information, personalized, fundraising) can map follower growth, it is especially important for information accounts and personalized accounts to do so. Given the nature of their Tweets, these accounts are a better barometer of true growth than fundraising accounts, which balloon and shrink based on whether they are engaged in a particular campaign. Because information accounts often have the best chance of being top of mind for journalists, mapping an account's increasing connections with influencers is an important metric as well.

## Tracking a Personalized Account

Accounts aiming for personalization also need to evaluate how they are doing. Here are some of the ways the three standard metrics in the T.W.E.E.T. model can be applied to evaluation of a personalized account:

- *Write: Quality*—Personalized accounts are often the most likely to not include media, links, and the like. For this reason, it's important to remember to add these in. Although followers tend to be more forgiving with frequent updates on personalized accounts, you should also look out for this, as some personalized accounts find that they are tweeting a bit too much for their followers' liking.

- *Engage: Retweets, @Replies*: Engagement in the form of @replies and retweets is an important part of tracking engagement for personalized accounts. Because it can be harder for personalized accounts to get retweets and @replies than it is for fundraising or information accounts, personalized accounts should try different tactics to lure followers into interacting. This is also an important place to watch out for the potential of integrating blogs or a dynamic homepage link. Personalized accounts are less likely to include links, so such additions can disconcert some followers at first. However, for long-term organizational success, integrating in more links will help up interest in the work of the non-profit.

- *Explore: Position, Growth*—Personalized accounts can be harder to grow, so looking at growth is an important metric to watch. Although information accounts easily place themselves on many lists, and fundraising accounts are preprogrammed for viral campaigns that will secure a certain number of followers, personalized accounts rely on the voice of the individual at the organization to maintain interest. Personalized accounts should keep an eye on how growth changes based on different tactics they use to try to gain followers.

## Tracking a Fundraising Account

• *Write: Quality, Activity*—Fundraising accounts face particular challenges with regularity and expectations. Firstly, they need to be sure to manage followers' expectations for what will happen when a particular campaign ends. Secondly, they need to prevent the account from going dormant when not in heavy promotion mode. Fundraising accounts will have weeks or months of higher activity (during a holiday fundraising push) and months with less activity (the middle of summer). It's important to work on improving during the holding pattern times.

• *Engage: Activity, Dollars Raised*—During any campaign, activity is one of the critical metrics, and for a fundraising campaign, dollars raised is a huge factor in engagement. Did the Tweets directly spur the followers to take the necessary action? This is a straightforward metric to track, for better or for worse.

• *Explore: Followers, Position, Growth*—For accounts that are interested in fundraising, follower growth can be trickier to track. Although (for the most part) the more followers one has, the better, there are other factors to consider. More followers will mean more eyeballs, but the issue with fundraising accounts is that they often grow during intense campaign times when individuals follow an account for the sole purpose of being part of a viral campaign—and not because they are necessarily genuinely interested in the account. For this reason, I think a more accurate metric for fundraising accounts is to ensure that their drop-off rate (that is, unfollowers) in the weeks following a big push are not too high, and that this rate goes down with each new campaign.

See an up-to-date list on the best ways to accept donations on Twitter at http://twitter4good.com/resources/processing-donations/

**WEB**

## Lessons Learned from a Twitterthon
by Diana Scimone, founder of Born2Fly.org

Born2Fly launched the 09/09/09 Twitterthon to raise money to stop child trafficking. Our goal was 9,000 people giving $9 each on 09/09/09—or $81,000. We didn't come close to raising that amount, but learned a lot about using social media tools like Twitter to promote and raise money for a cause. We used those insights to design our Twitterthon on 10/10/10. Our goal this time around was—you guessed it—10,000 people giving $10 each on 10/10/10. Here are the lessons we have learned:

### Build Your Base First
That's a key for any kind of fundraising, and it's no different for a social media fundraiser. We tried a very limited Twitterthon a few years ago, and it ended up with a big fail-whale on it—because I was new to Twitter and hadn't built any relationships. So I spent a year getting to know people and letting them know me. When it was time for 09/09/09, I didn't have to scramble to find retweeters or bloggers; they were there.

### Think Big, But Don't Set Your Goal in Concrete
Aim for somewhere between "gutter" and "Are you out of your mind?" On 09/09/09, I was so focused on raising $81,000 that

I missed the amazing point that raising over $20,000 in one day via social media was phenomenal. Those funds allowed us to pay for the pre-prep for the wordless book that's the centerpiece of The Born2Fly Project—illustrations, design work, professional scanning, and a lot more.

### Don't Focus on Your Goal

So we didn't raise $81,000 the first time out. What we got was even more valuable: an entirely new group of donors, many of whom have continued to give all year long. You can't get that kind of loyalty or enthusiasm by buying a mailing list.

### Widgets Work

ChipIn worked great for us in 2010. If someone makes a donation via the ChipIn widget on, for example, the Born2Fly website, the totals update on all the widgets throughout cyberspace.

### Don't Assume People Know What You've Been Working on 24x7

Late in the evening on 09/09/09, I DM'd a few people I assumed followed my every breath—and I was shocked to find they didn't even know about the Twitterthon. I thought I'd tweeted about it so much that Twitter was going to suspend my account for spamming—yet many of my followers didn't even know about it. So this year I DM'd and emailed my best contacts well ahead of time and asked if they would help retweet before the event and the day of the event.

### People Love Information

I knew people needed information about what child trafficking is, so I put together an info sheet. It gave them plenty of material to post on their blogs—or to use when writing their own stories. I did the same thing the following year, but incorporated it all into a news release format.

### Everyone Loves a Good Logo

Having our own 09/09/09 Twitterthon logo worked great (thank you, @cathleenkwas), and we did an update of it for 10/10/10 using the same font and overall design. We sent it to bloggers, media, and anyone who'd open the file. I started a separate Twitter account for the first event (@09–09–09), but it proved more trouble than it was worth, so I didn't do that again.

### People Need to Know What the Funds Will Be Used For

The more specific we can be about describing that, the better. We emphasized that once we finished testing the B2F educational materials in the Dominican Republic, we would begin distributing them all over the world to schools and organizations that have been patiently waiting for them. So we needed money to print and money to ship.

### Get Professional Help When You Need It

For 09/09/09 I worked with Christine Moore (@epiphanymediapr), who crafted an excellent, targeted news release that gained us a lot of exposure. For 10/10/10, I updated her release (and also worked with her to send it out to media). In September, @helpareporter (HARO) ran an ad for @prweb offering a free news release for new users. We jumped right on it, used most of what Christine wrote for us, and then scheduled it for release the week before the Twitterthon.

### Don't Sweat the Small Stuff

For 09/09/09, I spent far too much time getting prizes and then blogging about them to try to create excitement about the Twitterthon. For thirty days leading up to the event, I blogged about one of the prizes, linking back to the donating company and somehow connecting it to the fight to stop child trafficking. It was great to have prizes, and they did draw people, but when I factored in my time, the ROI was low.

### Major in Media

For 09/09/09, I spent a lot of time contacting digital media and got some excellent coverage. Having so much media coverage was huge and allowed us to go way beyond my own two-thousand-plus Twitter followers and the people on our mailing list. The following year I followed up with many of those same reporters; in some cases it worked and we got a repeat story, and in other cases it didn't.

### Ask What You Did Right—And What You Did Wrong

The week after 09/09/09, I emailed Tweeps (mutual followers) and bloggers who were especially helpful promoting the Twitterthon and asked for their feedback:

1. In your opinion, what worked? What didn't?
2. Any suggestions or ideas you'd like to share about B2F, the Twitterthon, or our future direction?
3. Would you like to stay involved with B2F—and if so, how?

When I was planning 10/10/10, I read through their replies and tried to incorporate them. The best piece of advice? From @jonswanson: "Celebrate what happened; it's a huge deal."

Jon is right. Although we didn't hit our financial goal, we hit many others we didn't even realize at the time. It was a huge deal.

## Tools to Track Effectively

To track effectively, you need access to the tools to do so. I asked Deanna Zandt, media technologist and author of *Share This! How You Will Change the World Through Social Networking,* about her three favorites:

- Rowfeeder
- Favstar
- Backtweets

As Zandt says, "Rowfeeder is a new one that I just love. Amazing metrics and extremely valuable for the price. Favstar is helpful for monitoring both people adding a

Tweet as a favorite, and retweeting (new style). Backtweets is another great tool—you can put in a URL, and no matter what it was shortened with, it'll show you who's tweeted it." Beth Kanter, author of *The Networked Nonprofit*, agrees that Rowfeeder is great—especially for events. She adds Twitalyzer to the list as a great way to measure the efficacy of your Tweets. Kevin Weil, product lead of revenue at Twitter, adds, "Twitter's advertising products, including Promoted Accounts and Promoted Tweets, can do a fantastic job of increasing your Twitter followers and helping to spread the word about your cause. Moreover, advertisers on Twitter can take advantage of advertiser-only, real-time analytics about their campaigns and accounts that measure their reach and ROI in a granular way." For those who aren't advertising, Weil says, "CoTweet can be an easy way to manage and analyze Twitter campaigns."

See a regularly updated list of the best tracking tools at http://twitter4good.com/resources/tracking-tools/ **WEB**

Finally, remember that tracking is about measuring results—but not necessarily quantitatively. Stories about the power of Twitter can be just as powerful in determining if your Twitter strategy is working. Marlon Parker is a social entrepreneur and mobile enthusiast passionate about using technology for social uplifting and empowerment. This passion was the reason for starting the non-profit Reconstructed Living Lab (RLabs), a social revolution enterprise using innovation and technology to bring about positive change in South Africa and beyond.

## The Twitter School
### By Marlon Parker

The Twitter School grew out of the increased interest in Twitter as a place for communication, learning, socializing, empowering, and just meeting great people. During the first school hosted by RLabs—a nonprofit headquartered on the Cape Flats in Cape Town, South Africa—Twitter was mostly used as an outlet to share messages of hope and give the members a voice. Most of the initial group [members] were ex-drug addicts and ex-gang members with no previous technology or media skills.

These ex-gangsters were now calling themselves "Twitter gangsters," also known as "Twitsters." One of the "Twitsters," aka @brent007, was an ex-gang leader and said he has more followers than he had when he was leading a notorious gang; now, through Twitter, he is able to leave positive footprints in the community he previously destroyed.

Twitter also became popular with disadvantaged women in the community, who were now being empowered to share their stories and to encourage one another. Since its inception in 2008, RLabs has hosted fourteen graduating classes and more than 650 pupils; many small community organizations are now leveraging the power of the platform.

What made these sessions exciting is the fact that the facilitators are all ex-pupils and community members from previous Twitter Schools. These classes were attended by a wide range of community members, from teenagers to the elderly, also presenting an opportunity for people in the community from different age groups to connect with one another on a personal level.

### Give Me My Daily Tweet
Initially all the Tweets within the group were from members encouraging one another and telling stories of hope to followers. We saw that those tweeting had experienced a major life transformation—evidenced not only by the stories they were sharing but also by the impact they were having offline. They were using Twitter not just as a news, media, and sharing online tool, but also as a gateway for positive messages that the group could

disseminate offline with family, friends, and the wider community. Many people were using Twitter as a medium to find messages of encouragement and hope to share with other members who are unable to access Twitter. One of the women, a single mother, said that Twitter is a place where she can connect with other mothers all around the world and draw strength from their messages.

### Tweeting My Way to Employment

In our community we have a high level of unemployment, with no industries around and many people living in poverty. Many of these community members have left school and are unable to fit back in the current schooling system. Through the Twitter schools, the community members were all passionate about using their Twitter skills. As they did so on a daily basis, an opportunity was birthed to address this major unemployment issue on the Cape Flats.

The trained community members who are unemployed were given opportunities to create extra income through being part of a social media team managing strategies for businesses, organizations, schools, and public figures. This meant that those organizations needing their social media strategy managed or outsourced not only got access to these services at very good prices but also gave mixed teams—consisting of experts and community members like our Twitsters and Twitter moms—an opportunity to work together and learn from each other. It's exciting when a single mom with no other form of income can use her Twitter skills and manage the Twitter stream for an organization via her mobile phone. She is then rewarded for each Tweet—and thus able to make a basic living through the RLabs employment program. Through this program RLabs is able to employ more than fifty community members, with half employed full-time.

### Twitter for Counseling

When community members are unable to access counseling service centers even as there is an increased adoption of Twitter, what better way to provide such services to people than through the platform itself? RLabs—in partnership with JamiiX, a contact center platform—was able to give people in need access to its advice and support services via Twitter. This meant that access to *live* support in the area of substance abuse, abuse, depression, stress and coping, and debt counseling was just a Tweet or instant message away. These services extended beyond just the Cape Flats; they reached the rest of Southern Africa, changing the lives of people one Tweet at a time.

### "Thank You, Twitter"

"I don't know what my life would be like if not for Twitter," says Monique (aka @shesthegeek and @moniqueross). A drug addict and suicidal just over three years before, Monique had nearly given up on life when she experienced a transformation and really fell in love with Twitter as an outlet for expressing herself. She was one of the first members of the Twitter School, and she is using Twitter effectively to encourage and empower other women. She also uses it as a tool to promote her technology brand "She's the Geek," giving women updates on what's happening in the technology space. Twitter has become part of Monique's daily diet; it is amazing to see how her life has changed in such a short period of time, from hopeless to hopeful, and she is always thankful for Twitter.

At RLabs, Twitter has become more than just a platform or a social media tool. To us it is not about the buzz, the hype, or the experts; it is about the people. Seeing lives being changed, hope being renewed, and people willing to walk the journey into their destinies is what Twitter means to the RLabs family. Although this movement started in the heart of the Cape Flats, it is now moving to other parts of Southern Africa and on to the whole of Africa.

## Becoming Streamlined

Streamlining is an essential part of the tracking plan. Once you have a system that is working, try to reduce the work involved so that you can get maximum results from minimal time output.

At the end of my training presentations, I used to show a slide meant to convey the concept of streamlining. I manage multiple accounts, and with each account I follow the

T.W.E.E.T. model laid out in this book. As a result, I have all manner of lists and saved searches for each of my Twitter profiles to keep up with Targeting, Writing, Engaging, Exploring, and Tracking. To me, my social media dashboard system is simple. To some audience members, however, it could not have been more terrifying. (Needless to say, I stopped using that slide.)

If you're a newbie used to following only your mom and your cat, the T.W.E.E.T. model will be more of a challenge than it is to social media veterans. Over time, though, you will find that you can streamline it such that you are spending the same amount of time on full social media immersion that you used to spend tracking Mom's and Fluffy's movements.

For some individuals, streamlining will mean outsourcing this work to someone else. The individual best poised to do the tweeting on behalf of your organization is typically someone within your organization. However, if this is not possible and you need to hire out for this, there are a couple of best practices to remember.

Firstly, ensure that you know what you are hiring for. If you are hiring someone to do the labor involved (the manual act of tweeting, @replying, and the like), do not hire someone who has his or her own fixed visions of what your Twitter target and strategy should be. Although there are many social media consultants who can help you develop an excellent Twitter target, this must be in done in tandem with the organization. In short, don't let go of the reins entirely. Have a plan, and make sure any outside hire sticks to it.

Deanna Zandt has worked with many organizations seeking to hire for this role, and she has served as this outsider herself many times in managing the accounts of other organizations. She is firm about the importance of outside consultants empowering the organization with the skills to work on their own in the future.

> For the most part, I'm of the "teach them to fish" school of consulting: I want my clients to absorb as much of my skills and knowledge as they can while they have me. Thus I make every effort to train and guide them into their own tweeting, if they're not doing it already. That said, there are certain campaigns where having an extra set of hands on deck to help with tweeting is useful—especially when there are huge time constraints and an organization's staff has to be focused on multiple prongs of the campaign's overall strategy. In that case, I spend a fair amount of time running potential Tweets by the client before the campaign gets going. This is really useful for them to see my style, and for me to understand theirs.

For example, one client of hers told her their brand didn't want to use exclamation points! Although that may have seemed a bit too specific, Zandt said, "It was true, and very helpful for me," adding, "Other than that, they pretty much trust me. I have a strong background in branding, and I think that helps me absorb the organizational voice quickly." She admitted that there are definite cons to the arrangement at times, and organizations should be aware of what it means to have an outsider come in: "The downsides are that it does take away from the authenticity of the conversation a little bit. It's almost like the difference between going to the Verizon store and going to the Authorized Reseller Verizon store. It's just not the same experience, no matter how good the consultant/freelancer is at quickly joining a team."

If the best way for your organization to maintain maximum efficacy is to hire an outside consultant to carry on your tweeting strategy, you should absolutely go ahead and do so. Just remember the importance of understanding and staying in control of the account's direction.

See more tips on hiring someone to help your organization with Twitter at http://twitter4good.com/resources/ hiring-twitter-help/

**WEB**

## Top Questions on the "Track" Step

Q: Where else can I learn more?

  A: There are a number of excellent resources out there that teach causes how to excel on the information network, and there is no better place to poke around for relevant teachers than on Twitter.

  See a complete list of some of my favorites in the "Book Resources" section on Twitter4Good.com.

**WEB**

  Be sure to also check out Twitter's Hope140.org, where we post case studies, how-to material, and information on the pro bono Promoted Tweets for Good program for causes and organizations.

  Finally, when tracking your progress, remember that what works in one country or community won't

always work in another. Alec Ross, senior advisor for
innovation to the U.S. secretary of state, says it well:

> What's been interesting to me in my international
> travels is not so much to see that Twitter is being
> used, but how it's being adopted and adapted
> locally. In certain places its more conversational,
> more like an open platform chat room, in other
> places it is more a mill for churning out press
> releases or official communiques. In other places
> it is used almost like a virtual world where one's
> identity in the offline world might bear very little
> resemblance to who they are on Twitter. Their
> Twitter persona is almost an avatar. It's really
> interesting. The larger point within all of this is not
> about Twitter per se but it's about how local com-
> munities adopt and adapt social media for their
> own purposes and their own contexts. If you look
> at the use of social media in Egypt for example, the
> fact that the tools were owned and developed out
> of California meant nothing to the people using
> them. They made those tools entirely their own
> and bent them to a point where they were legiti-
> mately Egyptian versus American or transnational.

Take note of how your organization tweets differ-
ently depending on where you are tweeting from, or
the constituents you are tweeting to, and monitor
what works.

Q: How long should it take each day to tweet?
  A: With a streamlined system, you can easily manage
     the Twitter accounts for your organization in two

twenty-minute blocks each day. You can certainly spend more time, but two twenty-minute periods are enough for you to adequately respond to @replies and direct messages, craft engaging Tweets, retweet and favorite others' Tweets, and complete the bulk of your other tasks on Twitter. Even if you have lots of followers, this is enough time.

Keep in mind that this does not include the time needed to develop your target in the beginning, find your particular voice in your writing, or find the initial list of influencers you want to follow and engage with. This also does not include extensive Twitter tangents—like reading every Tweet written by someone you may or may not have gone to high school with twenty years ago. For those journeys, the sky is the limit.

Q: What are other tips for streamlining my tweeting?

See a full list of productivity tips for using Twitter at
http://twitter4good.com/resources/productivity-tips/

**WEB**

A: Scheduling Tweets is a great way to help maintain a constant flow of Tweets—no matter what crisis your organization is dealing with in a given week. Additionally, if your non-profit organization docsn't want to worry about tweeting on holidays or weekends, it's extremely easy to schedule Tweets many months in advance. I often recommend Tweet scheduling; it works well as a way to highlight old content or information on your website, because this material is not time-sensitive. The main issue with Tweet scheduling is that you want to choose to schedule *only* those Tweets that are not time-sensitive. A great tactic is to use Tweet scheduling to focus on high-quality old information on your website that you want to make top of mind again for followers.

And of course, stay genuine when you schedule Tweets. Don't tell people you're having a "hard morning in the office" when you actually slept in late and are still at home. Finally, be careful about tweeting when you don't want to be "online." I sometimes schedule innocuous Tweets for days on which I know I won't be tweeting. On the day I turned in the final draft of this book, I knew I needed to be disconnected, so I scheduled a Tweet from earlier that week about a (bad) movie I saw. Word to the wise: if your book editor doesn't know you schedule your Tweets, she might think you're watching a movie and not finishing up your book manuscript!

3 hours ago via HootSuite

**@ClaireD**

The only thing in Tron that is unrealistic is that the video game company board meeting starts at midnight. #justsayin

http://twitter.com/#!/ClaireD/status/52134054379786240

# 7

# Applying the T.W.E.E.T. Framework

There is no magic bullet to excelling on Twitter, but there are clear, measurable ways to reach success. In this chapter we'll look at applying the entire T.W.E.E.T. model. By practicing the five key steps in the framework, we will see exactly how the model works to help organizations succeed.

## Case Study 1: Inua

Inua is a fictitious non-profit organization based in Nairobi, Kenya, that works to provide important services to pregnant, HIV-positive women who are facing extreme poverty. Inua, which means "uplift" in Kiswahili, is a 501(c)(3) non-profit organization that is registered in Boston but operates in ten women's centers throughout Nairobi. The centers house mothers during their pregnancies and in the months following; staff work on a case-by-case basis to help their clients. In addition to meeting the ongoing health needs of the women, education is a critical aspect of the curriculum in Inua's women's centers. Inua requires that all expectant mothers housed in the centers take courses to learn important skills to become better mothers, as well as pursue job-training classes to teach them to provide for their infants upon leaving the center. Inua also takes an active role in helping women with job placement and ongoing health issues for a period of two years after leaving the centers. The staff of Inua is composed of seven staff members based in Boston and over forty local staff in the ten women's centers. Inua receives most of its funding from private donors in the United States and has received several major multiyear grants from large foundations.

Inua had been on Twitter for three months when they realized they needed to concentrate on developing a real Twitter strategy; they had sent only a handful of Tweets during that time. For all intents and purposes, they felt they were making a fresh start when they decided to employ the T.W.E.E.T. model to get going.

## Target

The first step for Inua was to identify the Target for the account. Of the three main account Targets (information, personalized, fundraising), Inua was able to make a definite decision without too much difficulty. They chose a personalized account for a few reasons. First, when Inua had decided to begin using Twitter, they determined that the current staff member focused on communications (the director of communications) would be adding the role of Twitter strategy and management to her already full plate. As a result, Inua staff had concerns about the amount of time they could devote to Twitter, and they worried about their abilities to keep up with the (slightly) more demanding Target of being an information account. Additionally, fundraising on Twitter was not a present priority for Inua. Like most non-profits, they certainly needed funds, but they were currently the recipients of a large three-year grant, and they also had three annual events that raised significant funds for their organization. Based on time concerns, and for lack of an immediate fundraising goal, Inua decided to make their Target a personalized account.

They then identified five goals they hoped that this Target would help them reach within six months of implementing their strategy on Twitter. Although at first they were worried that all their goals were not measurable enough, they were confident that some of the clearest gains they could reap from Twitter would be more qualitative ones, so they wanted to include these in their list. Their five goals were

- To build a healthy following for the @inuaorg Twitter account so that when they sent an important Tweet, they could count on feedback from regular supporters. Although Kara, the director of communications (and now social media manager as well), knew that this was a somewhat "fuzzy" goal, it was one of the most important to her in identifying whether Twitter was working for Inua in their attempt to connect.

- To create a system whereby tweeting and managing the Twitter account takes no more than three hours a week. Kara knew her time was limited, and she calculated this was what she could devote to Twitter management.
- To make sure that more individuals in the community know about Inua's annual March walk-a-thon at the nearby high school, which typically raised more than $60,000 for the organization each year.
- To make international donors feel closer to the Kenyan women's centers and to give daily glimpses into life in the Nairobi centers.
- To draw more readers to Inua's blog, which featured local staff's video interviews with women in the Inua centers each month. In general, the blog was able to provide about four quality pieces a month (including a video interview), but its traffic was quite low, as the only current driver was the Inua monthly email newsletter.

Inua next mapped their organizational goals for the following six months alongside their Twitter Target. The March walk-a-thon was clearly a campaign they needed to involve Twitter in, and they worked on developing a specific campaign Target of fundraising for this particular effort while still sticking to the overall Target of having a personalized account. Although this might be a challenge, Kara felt that she had a naturally personal voice that would make it easy for her to tweet about fundraising activities and direct requests for funds while maintaining the account's personality.

## Write

With their Target in place, Inua next focused on getting down to the business of Writing. Although the social media manager, Kara, was excited about the personalized account Target, she did worry about the exact parameters of potential Tweets. What was *too* personal? Could she tweet about her commute? Her long holiday weekend? Trying to dive in without thinking too much, she began tweeting once a day while at work, retweeting and @replying multiple times a day, and sometimes scheduling Tweets for the weekends if she wasn't sure she'd be near a computer or on her mobile. She kept the material for the Tweets she scheduled focused on items that weren't time-sensitive or that didn't talk about being in the office if it was a Sunday, for instance. The following were the main types of Tweets that made up the @inuaorg timeline:

- Personal Tweets from Kara talking about what she was doing that day in the office, or (sometimes) on the road when she travelled to Kenya
- Personal Tweets from other staff members (only on occasion) that talked about their work from @inuaorg
- Tweets talking about new efforts that Inua was undertaking from Kara's point of view
- Individual @replies
- Tweets highlighting new content on the Inua blog

- Lots of retweeting—typically of Tweets written by two similar organizations operating in Nairobi that Inua regularly worked with

## Engage

At first, the engaging step came quite naturally to @inuaorg. Many of Inua's early followers were existing supporters who had already been on Twitter and were happy to see Inua embracing the platform; in the first few weeks they sent a flurry of @replies and direct messages to @inuaorg. Early engagement was very high, and Kara was pleased to see that with only a small following she was able to get good feedback quickly when she tweeted something out.

She was worried, though, about her existing donors and supporters getting bored once the novelty of Inua's entry onto Twitter had worn off, so she wanted to reach out to attract new followers. She set up a notification for every time a new follower followed her and then immediately followed them back, often even sending out an @reply immediately to thank them for their follow. Notably, though, she didn't set up an automatic reply. (I remember my first day at Twitter when I sat down next to Kevin Thau (@kevinthau) in business development. I told him my handle; he followed me, and then gently told me that my automatic @reply was a bit spammy. He was right.)

She saw an increase in followers, and when she put a note in her bio "@inuaorg will follow you back!" she saw a further spike. Soon, though, she was spending a lot of time sending @replies to new members. She had also started receiving irrelevant @replies that had nothing to do with Inua, and the levels of spammy @replies were rising as well.

## Explore

Inua was doing a couple of things to optimize their search for new accounts and influencers on Twitter. They had a regular dialogue on Twitter with two organizations in the Nairobi area they had worked with in the past, and Kara read the Tweets of these other two organizations religiously and retweeted them regularly. She also had automatic searches set up for terms like "Kenya" and "HIV/AIDS," but she hadn't found them very effective in leading her to new ideas. Mostly she just felt overwhelmed by the wealth of information coming in through these streams, and she frequently found herself spending too much time reading about a new AIDS awareness project in India, say, that had nothing to do with Inua. Honestly, time was a problem for her. She was spending so much time engaging with current followers that she didn't have many resources to devote to searching for new angles that Inua might explore on Twitter. Although she knew this was a concern, she couldn't see a way to fix it.

## Track

After six months of engaging in their new Twitter strategy, it was time for Inua to evaluate how far they had come. The first step was to look back at the five goals they had set for themselves and see where they stood now. Here are each of their original five goals compared with their current progress:

*Goal:* To build a healthy following for the @inuaorg Twitter account so that when they sent an important Tweet they could count on feedback from regular supporters.

*Progress:* Kara felt that they had done well on this goal, and even without a large following she did have good quality feedback and interactions. At times she felt that she had more interaction than she wanted (which we'll explore further). Although there was clearly always room for more growth (and more followers would help), she did feel confident that @inuaorg had made good strides in mostly accomplishing this.

*Goal:* To create a system whereby tweeting and managing the Twitter account takes no more than three hours a week. Kara knew her time was limited, and she calculated this is what she could devote to Twitter management.

*Progress:* On this goal, Kara didn't think @inuaorg had done so well. Frankly, she felt overwhelmed by Twitter. She loved it, but there was too much to do, and she didn't know what she should be focusing on anymore. She felt she was falling behind and couldn't catch up.

*Goal:* To make sure that more individuals in the community know about Inua's annual March walk-a-thon at the nearby high school, which typically raised more than $60,000 for the organization each year.

*Progress:* This goal had been met to some extent, and Inua had seen tons of Twitter activity on the days leading up to the big fundraiser. It was encouraging to see that so many Twitter users were also local supporters, and Kara thought that the passion of local supporters who were on Twitter was really helping to get other people who didn't know about Inua (and found them only on Twitter) interested in their work. She was excited about the prospects of integrating Twitter into future fundraising campaigns.

*Goal:* To make donors feel closer to the Kenyan women's centers and to give daily glimpses into life in the Nairobi centers.

*Progress:* Inua had achieved this to some extent, but Kara knew there was much room for improvement. Kara had a system of scheduling Tweets on the weekends, and she had been highlighting old posts on the blog that followers seemed to like. Kara also realized that this goal was very much tied into the goal about increasing traffic on the Inua blog. She knew there was a way to kill two birds with one stone on this, but was concerned about signing onto too much work—in terms of both blogging and tweeting—given that she was already strapped for time.

*Goal:* To draw more readers to Inua's blog, which featured local staff's video interviews with women in the Inua centers each month. In general, the blog was able to provide about four quality posts a month (including a video interview), but its traffic was quite low, as the only current driver was the Inua monthly email newsletter.

*Progress:* There was no question the Tweets Kara sent about the videos were popular and had increased traffic and engagement on the blog. Kara only wished she had more videos to post. But the videos took immense amounts of time for local staff to create, and it just wasn't feasible to do more than one or so a month. Kara also regretted at times forgetting to post the videos (or the other blog posts) right when they came out; sometimes she felt that posting a few days later was a disservice to the website.

Building off Kara's initial thoughts after reviewing the progress Inua had made so far on the five six-month goals, she then dove into some of the other metrics in the categories of Write, Engage, and Explore.

## Metric: Write

When faced with the long list of potential measurement points in the Write metric, a few stood out to Kara immediately as areas particularly relevant to the @inuaorg account:

- Best Tweet
- Worst Tweet
- Percentage of Tweets with media links
- Percentage of Tweets with photos

Without even doing any calculations of the number or percentage of Tweets she was sending with media links to video or photos, Kara knew it was very low. At the same time, she had seen again and again that her "best Tweets" were the ones that directed followers to watch the video of the month at the Inua blog. Putting these two facts together, she realized that @inuaorg simply had to start sending out more media, and had to do so in a way that also reached its aims of increasing blog traffic and letting overseas supporters feel more in touch with Inua's work in Kenya. In efforts to reduce the amount of work she would be taking on, Kara decided that a weekly photo feature was the way to go. The photo would be posted on the blog, increasing the number of monthly posts on the Inua blog from four to eight, and it would help serve all aims. It also wouldn't be hard. Inua had a backlog of amazing photographs taken over the past few years that could easily be used. Although photos were not as powerful as video, it was a good start. To make it easier on her, she also needed to set up an automatic RSS connect so that new blog posts would immediately get tweeted, without her having to remember to do so.

In looking at the category of "worst Tweet," Kara recalled that there had been a few times in the past six months when she had received particularly bad @replies in response to Tweets she had posted. Although the @replies weren't outright rude, they all suggested the same thing: Who cares about you waiting in line at the post office, Kara?

At the same time, Kara was looking at the actual numbers of Tweets (and the weekly averages) that the @inuaorg account had been sending out. In taking a good look at her Tweets over the past six month, Kara eventually realized that she had simply gotten too personal. In her efforts to not overedit herself, her Tweets had becoming increasingly ir-relevant to Inua's work, and they were also increasingly frequent. Although she had once tweeted once a day, she was now easily tweeting three to five times a day, and sometimes about (gasp!) what she was eating for lunch.

It was clear that she needed to begin editing her Tweets more and begin focusing on trying to make really powerful, personal statements. Additionally, it was time for her to create her own (very) personalized account. She obviously liked Twitter and the chance to share her thoughts with the world, but @inuaorg was not always the right place to do so. To reduce the few times that other employees were tweeting semi-personal messages from the @inuaorg account (making readers even more confused), she asked the rest of the Inua employees to set up personal Twitter accounts and to keep their Tweets on those streams. To help get @inuaorg back on the right track, and to remind followers what the account (and the organization) was all about, she also set up a monthly scheduled Tweet that simply explained the work of the organizations to new followers.

## Metric: Engage

Analyze what was retweeted, when, and why

- Number of retweets about your organization
- Most engaged day of the week
- Most engaged time of the day

Although some organizations focus too much on the number of retweets they are getting, Kara had clearly focused too little on this metric. No one was retweeting most of what she was saying, because most of it was not terribly connected to Inua and was a bit too personal for her followers' liking. If Kara focused more on a goal of getting retweeted, she would probably start crafting better Tweets. She decided she needed to start jotting down her ideas for funny and interesting Tweets that still gave a sense of Inua's work even when she was offline. When she logged on, she could look at this list and pick a good one, instead of saying whatever (bad) Tweet came to her in any given harried moment.

When faced with looking at the days and times of most engagement on the @inuaorg account, Kara came to another startling conclusion. Aside from @replies (which sometimes were irrelevant), the biggest problem she saw with her engagement was that her followers seemed present, and liked to @reply, but for the most part they weren't really engaged *in anything*. They were there, waiting and listening, but she wasn't asking them to do anything. To fix this, she decided to start a weekly question with its own hashtag: #upliftaids. By sending out a specific question related to Inua and to the larger global issue of HIV/AIDS, Kara hoped she would be able to focus her followers' engagement on a productive meme, or weekly feature. She experimented, using questions like "How much does a year of ARV treatment cost in the USA compared to Kenya?" Along the same lines, she realized she had to become more proactive about asking for engagement. She vowed to scan through her follower list to find individuals who looked like they had a big reach and to specifically ask them to retweet certain messages.

## Metric: Explore

Kara's idea about asking influential followers to retweet her messages brought up another question: Did she even have many influencers to reach out to in the first place who were already following @inuaorg? To explore this a bit more, she evaluated a couple of key areas:

- Number of lists following (lists your organization is following)
- Number of lists created (lists your organization created)
- Size and growth of lists created
- Number of influencers actively on to-follow PR list
- New relationships created

When Kara looked at the list of potential metric points to better understand how she was doing on the Explore step, she knew she had a lot of work to do. Inua needed influencers, and she simply had to make this a priority in the next six months. She saw that she was spending all her time interacting with existing followers (some of whom were hardly quality followers at all). Although it is important for non-profit organizations to not ignore their loyal supporters, Kara had taken this to an extreme. She was tweeting in a bubble (and sometimes in a bubble with spammers); she needed to branch out. She immediately set a goal for herself to spend all her allotted Twitter time for the coming week using the tips in the Explore chapter (Chapter Five) to look for relevant influencers, follow them, and create public (and private) lists of them as necessary. She knew that the support of a true Twitter influencer could be one of the biggest wins for the @inuaorg account, and she decided once and for all to give this task the time it deserved.

She also knew there were other areas of exploring that demanded attention. For example, she needed to search more regularly for mentions of @inuaorg. Kara was sure she had set up an automatic stream searching for mentions of Inua on Twitter, but she couldn't find it to save her life; she assumed it had gotten deleted during one of her frantic days of @replying thirty people who probably had only questionable interest in Inua. She put this on her list of must-dos. Her list didn't end there, though; she knew there was a lot in the area of exploring that she had to do. She wanted to find a role model non-profit organization account to follow; another good step would be to apply for Twitter's pro bono Promoted Tweets for Good at Twitter's Hope140.org.

Although it had taken some time to truly evaluate the @inuaorg account and what it had accomplished in the preceding six months, it had been a productive exercise, and Kara felt much clearer on what needed to be focused on next. Using what she had learned, she drew up a list of five goals for the next six months, largely related to refining her tweeting and ensuring that the majority of her time was spent engaging with true influencers. In this way, she hoped to move forward.

I created the fictional organization of Inua to represent many of the modern concerns of non-profit organizations wanting to make a difference on Twitter. This case study addresses many key issues, including the following:

- *Inua is international.* Inua reminds readers that non-profit organizations around the globe can use the tools in this book to excel, and that success on Twitter is not dependent on proximity to Silicon Valley.
- *Inua does not have a large following.* @inuaorg shows how you can gain just as much benefit from Twitter as some of the mega-organizations with millions of followers.
- *Inua juggles many concerns all at once.* This case also brings up multiple issues regularly facing organizational accounts, including fundraising, active volunteers, multimedia tweeting, blog and website traffic concerns, conveying sensitive information, and invoking personality in Tweets.

Ultimately, Inua represents a non-profit organization working to make an impact via Twitter without massive resources. Many readers of *Twitter for Good* will identify with their strong mission, limited means, and occasional feelings of overwhelm on their journey.

Now let's look at another example of how we can use the T.W.E.E.T. model, this time in a cause-driven, for-profit setting.

## Case Study 2: Viva

Viva is a large Latin American television station based in Caracas, Venezuela, that hosts a variety of daytime and evening programming. Apart from talk shows, news programs, hosted variety shows, and game shows, Viva is most known for hit soap operas (*telenovelas*). Caracas is a hub for the telenovela industry, and of all the products Viva produces, telenovelas are the most widely translated and distributed to other television networks throughout the world. A twenty-five-year-old organization, Viva has nearly six hundred employees in eight countries. More than half work in Caracas.

Although Viva has always been involved in giving back to the local communities, the past five years has seen a formalizing of the company's charitable work under the arm of the Fundación Vivir Bien (Live Well Foundation). The small foundation has one full-time staff member whose primary role is to coordinate an annual one-month healthy living campaign that provides donations to third-party non-profits centered on healthy living. This staff member works extremely closely with the rest of the Caracas-based Viva staff to create a packed month of charitable activities that include a live televised music concert to raise funds from the general public, airing of dozens of public service messages filmed by high-profile actors and actresses at Viva, and the airing of a short documentary explaining how the work of the previous year's campaign was able to positively impact local healthy living initiatives in Latin America. Historically Viva has funded the campaign itself, but in the past few years it has begun to broker deals with snack food companies promoting healthy products via Viva on-air talent during the campaign. These outside funds allow Viva to create a broader television awareness campaign and provide more direct aid to the non-profit beneficiaries.

Although Viva is a high-profile TV station in Latin America that many individuals talk about on Twitter, the organization has done little proactively to take the reins of Twitter themselves and truly direct their own strategy. About a year ago, Sol, the social media manager based in Caracas, signed up for Twitter with the account @vivaviva and encouraged two colleagues (one in Mexico City and one in Madrid) who dealt with marketing in those regions to also sign up as @vivavivamx and @vivavivaes. To date, these are the three semi-official Viva Twitter channels that Sol is aware of. However, many individual employees have their own accounts, as do a host of the individual actors, actresses, and hosts affiliated with Viva.

In applying the T.W.E.E.T. model, Sol knew she would have to streamline many of these different accounts, and she wanted to get started.

## Target

First, Viva identified its Target. Sol focused first on finding a Target for the main account, @vivaviva.

Of the three main account Targets (Information, Personalized, Fundraising), she was able to easily decide on an *information account*. The company simply had too many individuals involved (not to mention a public relations team still getting used to the idea of Twitter) to make a personalized account viable. Plus, as a TV station with more than forty weekly programs and dozens of well-known Latin American actors, the one thing they never lacked was information. Because the focus of the campaign was more on awareness than on fundraising, a fundraising account was also not their top choice.

Viva (with Sol taking the lead) then identified five goals they hoped this Target would help them achieve within six months of implementing their strategy on Twitter:

- To create a database of all Viva-related accounts, including accounts that represent Viva's individual television shows, individual talent accounts, general Viva accounts, and all personal staff accounts. The goal would be to not only track these, but also to ensure that these accounts were provided with reliable messaging to help support the healthy living campaign.
- To streamline the "main" Viva accounts by eliminating impersonation accounts, inactive accounts, and otherwise nonessential accounts so that the main Viva handles had clear owners and goals. Each of these main accounts then needed a plan and a schedule to ensure it was providing the relevant information required for both Viva as a television station and Viva's healthy living initiative.
- To provide Twitter training to staff and talent, and to find a balance between suggesting best practices to Viva-related employees when tweeting and not restricting their individual expression.
- To bring Viva's Twitter presence on-air, and to do so through the healthy living campaign. Although many other TV stations had begun incorporating Twitter,

Viva had been slow to do so, mostly because of their late arrival on the platform.

- To create individual Twitter accounts for each market devoted to conveying show times and market-specific information.

Mapping Viva's goals for the healthy living campaign next to their Twitter target, they knew that the healthy living campaign would remain present throughout the year, but would have a particular focus during its one-month push—when it would take precedence on the @vivaviva account.

## Write

Although it was clear to Sol that Viva should certainly be an information account, her first challenge was in trying to decide what kind of information should go into the @vivaviva Twitter stream. The sheer quantity of information was overwhelming. There were forty programs a week to (potentially) talk about, and dozens of actors and actresses—many with their own Twitter handles. Trying to dive in without thinking too much, Sol began tweeting once a day while at work, retweeting and @replying multiple times a day, and sometimes scheduling Tweets for the weekends if she wasn't sure she'd be near her computer or mobile. She kept the material for the Tweets she scheduled focused on items that weren't time-sensitive, or that didn't talk about being in the office if it was a Sunday, for instance.

## Engage

When a large brand comes on Twitter for the first time, their experience is very different from that of a small organization. Instead of working to make a name for themselves—and trying to start a conversation—their task is to engage with the conversations already under way. @vivaviva didn't need to carve its own space on Twitter so much as it needed to find the niche it had already been allocated, and then start speaking up. Given the nature of @vivaviva as a television station with many high-profile actors, Sol quickly found that people were talking about Viva all over Twitter. As an information account, she saw her role as one of providing quality, "official" information in the many settings where people were already talking about Viva, Viva programs, or Viva actors and actresses. To do this, Sol had to remind herself frequently to make sure her interactions accurately reflected the brand that Viva had crafted over the past twenty years.

Another issue Sol faced was the amount of interaction she saw that the fans wanted. As soon as @vivaviva became active on Twitter, even more fans came out of the woodwork, and Sol couldn't keep up with the flurry of @replies, direct messages, and hashtags directed at @vivaviva. Sol realized that, as an information account, @vivaviva didn't need to interact with everyone; rather, her job, given her Target, was to create valuable, fresh information that made fans feel connected—even if she couldn't connect with everyone individually.

## Explore

When @vivaviva first implemented the T.W.E.E.T. model, the best they could do on the Explore step was simply to find and keep up with the massive amount of information already out there on Twitter about the company, their actors, their television programs, and their healthy living initiatives. Although Viva hadn't been active on Twitter for the past few years, *others* had been actively tweeting about them—and they needed to make sure that they were following these conversations to help better manage their brand.

## Track

After six months of engaging in their new Twitter strategy, it was time for Viva to evaluate how far they had come. The first step was to look back at the five goals they had set for themselves and see where they stood. Here are each of their original five goals compared with their current progress:

*Goal:* To create a database of all Viva-related accounts, including accounts that represent Viva's individual television shows, individual talent accounts, general Viva accounts, and all personal staff accounts. The goal would be to not only track these, but also to ensure that these accounts were provided with reliable messaging they could use to help support the healthy living campaign.

*Progress:* Despite the massive undertaking it had been to find all Viva-related accounts, Sol was particularly pleased with the result of having a database of all these accounts.

She was able to organize them into different Twitter lists, encourage everyone to follow and retweet each other, and make sure that no one was tweeting in a bubble. When it came time to rally around the healthy living campaign, this was more important than ever. She saw this as a big win.

*Goal:* To streamline the "main" Viva accounts by eliminating impersonation accounts, inactive accounts, and otherwise unimportant accounts so that the main Viva handles had clear owners and goals. Each of these main accounts then needed a plan and a schedule to ensure that it was providing the relevant information required for both Viva as a television station, and Viva's health living initiative.

*Progress:* Sol had faced a massive challenge in cleaning up the mess that Viva had created with its dozens of errant, inactive Twitter accounts, and by the time she was (mostly) done with this task she well knew the downside to having too many accounts that you can't keep up with. Sol vowed to never encourage this again. She focused on one main Viva account, @vivaviva, that could provide all outward-facing communication from the company and the foundation. It would include anything connected to Viva programming, as well as anything related to the healthy living campaign. To deal with the forty individual TV shows on the Viva lineup that each had their own Twitter handles, she wrote memos to the individual television programs seeking owners for the accounts. Owners would need to update at least once a week; if they couldn't, the account would be cut. In the end, she ended up with about twenty shows that wanted to go forward with individual Twitter accounts, promising frequent updates.

*Goal:* To provide Twitter training to staff and talent, and to find a balance between suggesting best practices to Viva-related employees when tweeting and not restricting their individual expression.

*Progress:* This goal had been met to some extent, in that Sol had done a PowerPoint presentation to the Caracas staff that gave them basic Viva-flavored Twitter onboarding tips. Specifically, she had provided suggestions about promoting @vivaviva, using Viva-created hashtags, tweeting about Viva talent, and following Viva lists. She had also dispersed several memos with this information to the other Viva offices outside of Caracas. Some staff members did learn the best practices, of course, but many also complained that Viva was trying to shape the messaging of what were essentially their personalized accounts. Ultimately, Sol gave up on trying to do much with personalized employee accounts; she hoped that their enthusiasm for their work and the healthy living campaign would create organic Tweets about the topics. She focused instead on working directly with some of her higher-profile actors and actresses on Twitter. If they were able to send out better messaging even some of the time, that would prove a bigger win.

*Goal:* To bring @vivaviva's Twitter presence on-air, and to do so through the healthy living campaign. Although many other TV stations had been doing this, Viva had been slow to do so, mostly because of their own slowness on the platform.

*Progress:* As soon as Sol, with the backing of the marketing director, was able to convey that there would be a new push to drive Twitter followers and engagement, she found that most Viva talent easily stepped up to the plate to more aggressively use and promote @vivaviva's use of Twitter on-air. Sure, there were some who didn't want to use the platform and worried about their privacy, but she was amazed how many had already embraced it and saw tweeting about the healthy living campaign as a natural extension of tweeting about what they were doing every day, anyway. In this area, she couldn't help but kick herself, feeling like Viva had wasted a few years not taking advantage of this kind of extra (free) promotion from these high-profile actors and actresses.

*Goal:* To create individual Twitter accounts for each market devoted to conveying show times and market-specific information.

*Progress:* Although Sol still believed this was a good goal, she ultimately decided not to move forward with it. All the work of cleaning up the inactive accounts and streamlining the Viva brand on Twitter had showed her how detrimental it was to their brand to have lots of inactive or poor-quality accounts. She did believe it would benefit local viewers to have relevant local information, but she knew the focus right now should be on promoting the overall Viva message on Twitter. She finally had a strategy in mind, and she didn't want to begin dividing up potential followers into multiple, less than stellar accounts. Additionally, she believed that there simply were no hands available to maintain these local area accounts effectively. Maybe this could be revisited down the road.

Through this process, Sol had also found out how many of the healthy living campaign sponsors were already on Twitter. This made it easy to have talent mention their Twitter handles and the handles of the brands or products they were promoting online, and it created an instant offline connection between the viewer and the healthy living campaign. Throughout the course of the campaign, Sol was able to work directly with their major sponsoring brands and beneficiary non-profits; she had a custom Twitter background designed to reinforce the image of a united front on Twitter.

Sol then began to look at some of the other metrics within the T.W.E.E.T. framework steps of Write, Engage, and Explore to get a complete sense of what they had learned in their first months of implementation.

## Metric: Write

In terms of Tweet crafting and creation, Sol immediately identified these metrics as relevant in terms of the success of @vivaviva:

- Response to different types of Tweets
- Percentage of Tweets linking to the organization website
- Existing memes

Like Kara and @inuaorg, Sol decided that @vivaviva needed to take better advantage of the ability to use media in their Tweets. Although it would take some legwork to ensure that all the on-air public service spots the actors and actresses filmed for the healthy living campaign could go on the Viva website, Sol knew this was crucial. With these clips—and with much of their other on-air content—@vivaviva had the potential to rally followers around a video that they hoped would go viral. Because they're a TV station, video was their huge asset, and they simply weren't engaging with it on Twitter as much as they could be. Encouraging videos in Tweets would have the added result of sending more people to the Viva website to watch even more.

Sol also was looking for ways to increase Viva's efforts to connect live tweeting of on-air talent, tweeting of viewers, and the @vivaviva Twitter account. She decided that creating a Viva-specific meme on Twitter would be a good idea. With something like #vivamejor ("live better"), Sol could encourage the various television programs, actors, and actresses to not only use the hashtag on their Twitter accounts when mentioning ways to live more healthily, but to also talk about the hashtag on-air. It would pull together the on-air and off-air Twitter elements and spark greater engagement with fans during the healthy living campaign.

## Metric: Engage

To Sol, increased followers would indicate the reach of her campaign; this was a key metric point for @vivaviva. A few other points were also of particular interest:

- Number of followers
- Reach of a Tweet
- Most engaged time of the day

Because they had chosen the Target of an information account, she knew that her followers didn't necessarily come for her voice or her personal responses, but rather for the content and the brand that Viva represented—and this was more important than ever while promoting the healthy living campaign. Viva's great asset was the reach of its on-air programming and talent. Sol was consistently working with their stars to help them promote the healthy living initiatives from @vivaviva, and she knew it was important to isolate which of their talent were most effective at reaching interested parties. Once she saw some of her efforts begin to pay off—and the effectiveness of on-air promotion in converting new followers—she began to experiment with the best time of day to send Tweets in her efforts to optimize.

## Metric: Explore

There were a few metrics in particular within the Explore category that gave Sol a wake-up call about some of the work still to be done.

- Press mentions of Twitter account
- New relationships created
- Number of lists following (lists your organization is following)
- Number of influencers actively followed

For a large brand like Viva—and a large account like @vivaviva—it was easy to forget all that she might be missing by not spending more proactive time on this step. Indeed, when Sol looked back at the past six months, she saw there was little time for exploring anything. Viva has the huge asset of a large base of potential Twitter users who could generate large followings (because some were high-profile, and because of the sheer volume of accounts between individual TV shows, actors, and the main Viva channel account itself). In truth, after six months she was still catching up. Although she saw the concept of exploring as valuable, and she tried to start tweeting some important Latin American TV journalists from the @vivaviva account, she knew this was an area she would need to work on.

In the future, Sol would need to take the advice that Kara from the Kenyan non-profit organization was already following—rereading the Explore chapter of this book (Chapter Five), looking for relevant influencers, following them, and creating public (and private) lists of them as necessary.

The Viva case study brings up many issues that brands regularly face when they buckle down to start making a difference using Twitter. By starting on Twitter before they made a *decision* (or devised a strategy) to do so, they don't know their own strengths.

Ultimately, both of these case studies show organizations that believe in the power of Twitter to reach their supporters but need help to do so well. Although they each have a ways to go, they are trying hard to educate their followers and change the world. For a small non-profit organization like Inua, using the T.W.E.E.T. model can be an effective, concrete way to better prepare a winning strategy and excel on Twitter. A large brand like Viva has just as much potential to benefit from the T.W.E.E.T. framework.

See more great case studies of organizations using the T.W.E.E.T. model at http://twitter4good.com/resources/case-studies/

# Conclusion

Twitter can be an immensely powerful tool for organizations that want to make a difference in the world. The key is learning the most effective way to use the real-time information network to meet these aims. In *Twitter for Good*, we've explored how any organization can best excel on Twitter using a straightforward and effective framework. The mission of Twitter—to promote open information—is at the heart of cause-based work, and my hope is that my model will help you reach these aims.

Twitter works because it is simple and easy to use. The barrier to entry is low, and the potential for impact is high. As such, it levels the playing field for change activation. In turn, the T.W.E.E.T. framework is modeled after the very platform it was built for. Innovative, instinctive, and practical, it marries best practices with basic usability. Learning to use Twitter well is not a science, but an ongoing lesson. Using the T.W.E.E.T. framework is a similar process.

As you begin to apply what you've learned in this book, I hope you will bear two things in mind. First, recall that Twitter is much more than a social media network; rather, it's a global real-time information network—and every day, you and your organization are newsworthy. Second, remember that the key to success on Twitter is in the T.W.E.E.T. (Target, Write, Engage, Explore, Track). By remembering these two things, you will be well on your way to changing the world, one Tweet at a time.

# Top Questions Reference List

Here, in one location, are the top questions that I answer at the ends of Chapters Two through Six.

## Chapter 2

- What if I choose the wrong Target for my organization's account?
- How can I identify the Target choices of existing organizations on Twitter so that I can get a better feel for what the three main goals look like in practice?
- Does the choice of which individual will tweet from my organization's account affect the Target I choose?

## Chapter 3

- Who should write the Tweets?
- Who should *send* the Tweets?
- How often should I tweet?

- Can I delete a Tweet?
- Should I geotag my Tweets?
- Should I send automatic feeds for picture, video, or blog posts to Twitter? If I do send automatic RSS feeds, should I do so on all my social networks or just one?

## Chapter 4

- What if someone says something negative about my organization?
- Who should monitor my organization's Twitter account?
- Are Twitter parties a good way to promote engagement?
- What about Tweet-ups?
- All these suggestions are well and good, but what I really need is *one million followers*. Once I have *one million followers*, then I'll start implementing your ideas. *Can you help me get one million followers?*

## Chapter 5

- How do I find the influencers?
- Once I find the influencers, what's the best way to contact them via Twitter?

## Chapter 6

- Where else can I learn more?
- How long should it take each day to tweet?
- What are other tips for streamlining my tweeting?

# Resources

www.Twitter4Good.com

www.Hope140.org

www.ClaireDiazOrtiz.com

Twitter for Good *Book Companion Resources:*

A list of examples of information accounts at http://twitter4good.com/resources/information-accounts/

A list of examples of personalized accounts at http://twitter4good.com/resources/personalized-accounts/

A list of examples of fundraising accounts at http://twitter4good.com/resources/fundraising-accounts/

A list of popular memes at http://twitter4good.com/resources/memes/

Top tips on finding a great Twitter role model for your case at http://twitter4good.com/resources/role-model/

An example of a Twitter campaign planning chart at http://twitter4good.com/resources/plan-your-twitter-campaign/

A full list of some of the best Tweets of all time at http://twitter4good.com/resources/best-tweets/

More tips on integrating Twitter with your organizational blogging efforts at http://twitter4good.com/resources/blogging/

A list of some great hashtags to follow at http://twitter4good.com/resources/hashtags/

A list of some of the best questions to ask your Twitter followers at http://twitter4good.com/resources/best-questions/

More information about Twitter parties at http://twitter4good.com/resources/twitter-parties/

A list of some of the best blogs focused on Twitter at http://twitter4good.com/resources/best-twitter-blogs/

An up-to-date list on the best ways to accept donations on Twitter at http://twitter4good.com/resources/processing-donations/

A regularly updated list of the best tracking tools at http://twitter4good.com/resources/tracking-tools/

More tips on hiring someone to help your organization with Twitter at http://twitter4good.com/resources/hiring-twitter-help/

A full list of productivity tips for using Twitter at http://twitter4good.com/resources/productivity-tips/

More great case studies of organizations using the T.W.E.E.T. model at http://twitter4good.com/resources/case-studies/

# Acknowledgments

Every day, I am lucky to help other organizations learn how to best use Twitter. Biz Stone and his vision for changing the world got me here, and dozens of other Twitter employees have given of their time and energy to boost me at various stages in my role leading corporate social innovation, causes, and philanthropy at Twitter. Thanks to many, including @biz, @ev, @dickc, @jack, @katies, @jbuckhouse, @abdur, @jennadawn, @laura, @sg, @mgrooves, @cpen, @jillyface, @choppedonion, @del, @francesca, @elizabeth, @jess, @goldman, @chloes, @adambain, @mgrooves, @cpen, @bakari, @ali, @omid, @briggles, @crystal, @olivia, @omid, @janetvh, @amac, @mgale, @gregpass, @kris, @anm, @dougw, @kevinthau, @kevinweil, @seacue, and many, many more.

Twitter is a fabulous company, and I could not be prouder to work here as it grows and changes, even if I do sometimes lament the demise of the Monday breakfast burrito.

Outside of Twitter, amazing support came from many individuals who contributed thoughts, essays, and quotes to the text about their experiences changing the world on Twitter. Thanks to John Wood, Darren Rowse, Nick Kristof, Amalia McGibbon, Amanda Rose, Beth Kanter, Leila Janah, Mark Horvath, Luke Renner, April Rinne, Alec Ross, Marlon Parker, Christie George, Craig Newmark, Rebecca Hankin, Tim Ferriss, Kelly Creeden, Melanie Mathos, Katie Dowd, Lynette Camara, Lara Vogel, Deanna Zandt, Christie George, Jessica Shortall, Samuel Ikua Gachagua, Laura Vanderkam, Patrick Meier, Chrysi Philalithes, Laura Adams, Tara Roth McConaghy, Patrick Meier, Jon Gosier, Scott Stratten, Catherine Connors, Suzanne Hall, Abby Falik, Wil Keenan, Gretchen Steidle Wallace, Raymond Nasr, Adam Rugel, Cindy Tanaka, James Kondo, Carrie Isaac, Ron Conway, and Chris Sacca. I would not be where I am today were it not for generous support from both the Skoll Foundation and the Skoll Centre for Social Entrepreneurship at Oxford University's Said Business School. Thanks to Jeff Skoll, Sally Osberg, Pamela Hardigan, Alex Nichols, and Kim Alter, among others.

Many thanks go to those behind this book-making machine. The wise counsel of Byrd Leavell at the Waxman Agency has made these five years fly by and has given me reason to be glad I ever tried my hand at this whole writing thing. My excellent editor, Karen Murphy at Jossey-Bass, turned my harried words into wise teachings, and made South by Southwest a joy, to boot. Mary Garrett and

John Maas also did much to help. Ellen Gerstein of Wiley sparked it all.

Although this was not my first book, it was my fastest. The swift writing journey could not have happened without the selflessness of José Díaz Ortiz to step up as CEO of our new family during a frighteningly busy season. I wrote; he did everything else. Love and humble thanks abound.

Like all good teenagers, Sammy sent me snow day pictures when he should have been studying for finals. Like all good guardians, Lara gave him menacing looks on my behalf. (Brava!)

Barb and Lance were gracious last-minute hoteliers, never failing to ask, after a long hard day, "How's the tweeting?" Court was a hygienic chauffeur to my solo writing retreat, and Little Tony, in true form, stole my kombucha.

All errors are mine, although I'd rather you blame someone else.

If I do say so, it's been a good Tweet.

# About the Author

**Claire Díaz-Ortiz** (née Williams) leads social innovation and philanthropy at Twitter, where she has worked since 2009.

She is a frequent international speaker and is known for developing the T.W.E.E.T. model—a framework to help organizations and individuals best excel on Twitter.

Claire holds an MBA from Oxford University, where she was a Skoll Foundation Scholar for Social Entrepreneurship. She also holds a bachelor's degree and a master's degree from Stanford University.

She is the cofounder of Hope Runs (www.HopeRuns .org), a non-profit organization operating in Kenya, and owner of Do Well Media (www.DoWellMedia.com).

Claire has lived on four continents and travelled to more than fifty countries. She has been widely written about in such publications as *Business Week*, the *Independent* and the *Huffington Post*.

*Twitter for Good* is her second book.

Find more from Claire at www.ClaireDiazOrtiz.com and on Twitter via @ClaireD.

# Index

ML          1/12